HOLY TRINITY,
PERFECT COMMUNITY

HOLY TRINITY, PERFECT COMMUNITY

Leonardo Boff

*Translated from the Portuguese
by Phillip Berryman*

ORBIS BOOKS

Maryknoll, New York 10545

Originally published as *Santíssima Trindade é a melhor communidade*,
copyright © 1988 by Leonardo Boff, by Editora Vozes Ltda, Rua Frei
Luís, 100, 25689-900 Petrópolis, RJ, Brasil.

Translation copyright © 2000 by Orbis Books.

Published by Orbis Books, Maryknoll, NY 10545-0308.

Scripture quotations are from the New Revised Standard Version Bible,
copyright © 1989, by the Division of Christian Education of the Na-
tional Council of the Churches of Christ in the United States of America.

Manufactured in the United States of America.

Manuscript editing and typesetting by Joan Weber Laflamme.

Library of Congress Cataloging-in-Publication Data

Boff, Leonardo.
    [Santíssima Trindade é a melhor comunidade. English]
    Holy Trinity, perfect community / Leonardo Boff ; translated from
the Portuguese by Phillip Berryman.
        p. cm.
    ISBN 1-57075-332-6 (pbk.)
    1. Trinity. 2. Sociology, Christian. 3. Liberation theology. I. Title.

BT111.2.B64 2000
231'.044—dc21

To Marcia Miranda,
mother of six children,
lay theologian, companion in struggle,
for her communion with the oppressed,
concrete expression of the communion
of the Father, Son, and Holy Spirit.

Contents

I

In the beginning is the communion of the Three not the solitude of a One

II

The revealing of the Trinity

III

Human reason and the Blessed Trinity

IV

Human imagination and the Blessed Trinity

V

What the Blessed Trinity is:
Communion of life and love among the divine Three

VI

The communion of the Trinity:
Critique and inspiration for society and church

VII

The Person of the Father:
Mystery of tenderness

VIII

The Person of the Son:
Mystery of communication and principle of liberation

IX

The Person of the Holy Spirit:
Mystery of love, and in-breaking of the new

X

The Trinity in heaven and the Trinity on earth: The internal history of the Trinity reflected in the external history of creation

Preface

At the root of all great human problems there always lies a theological issue. There is always a demand for what is radical, in the sense of a final meaning, an ultimate reference point. Anyone taking up such questions becomes a theologian, regardless of whether he or she belongs to a religion or confession, or uses the technical terminology devised by what is called theology. The questions are unavoidable: What is the ultimate structure of being? What is hidden behind what we see, live, and suffer? What can we hope for? Is there some ultimate shelter? Who will take us in?

The answers to such existential and social questions are codified by religions. Theologies seek to give them legitimacy using all the resources of reason and other means of persuasion. This institutional character notwithstanding, each human being asks these questions and seeks a response that will fit his or her perception of reality.

Each type of society tends to produce a religious representation suited to it. The dominant religion in a group is the religion of the dominant group. The dominant form of the representation of God is influenced by the way the dominant culture represents God, and it does so in the framework of its fundamental interests. Thus, in a capitalist society—which is based on individual performance, private accumulation of goods, and the predominance of the individual over the social—the representation of God usually accentuates the fact that God is one alone, Lord of all, all-powerful, the source of all power. The usual conclusion is that those who wield power on earth are God's natural representatives. The

Mongol Mangu Khan wrote a letter to the king of France expressing such logical reasoning: "This is the order of the eternal God; in heaven there is one eternal God and on earth there will be only one master, Genghis Khan, the son of God." His seal reads, "One God in heaven and Khan on earth, seal of the Master of the earth."

As an institution in history, the church has developed within the Western framework, which is strongly marked by the concentration of power in a few hands. It has been inculturated into settings where monarchical power, the principle of both authority and property, prevailed over other values more oriented toward community and society. That provides a basis for understanding the current historical profile of the church institution and how it distributes religious labor between clergy and laity, with remarkably little participation. In such a context people are unlikely to assimilate the trinitarian mystery as the communion of three distinct Persons, who, while distinction is maintained, are, out of love and communion, one sole God. A trinitarian doctrine based on the unity of the single divine nature or the figure of the Father, sole cause and ultimate source of the entire godhead, will be presented as the one most suited to the general context of the culture. It is not surprising, then, that the prevailing mindset in the church is more that of an "a-trinitarian" or "pre-trinitarian" monotheism than a true trinitarian consciousness of God. Returning to a radically trinitarian understanding of God would help the church overcome the clericalism and authoritarianism that are still very much in evidence in ecclesiastical behavior. What challenges the structure of a church that still concentrates too much power in the clergy is actually not so much secularization or the politicization of faith—these are lesser risks—but to live out trinitarian faith as communion among those who are different and so form a living and open community.

Such faith would lead the entire church structure toward a conversion process. The very structure would be evangelized because Puebla[1] was on the mark when it taught that "evangelization is a call to participation in trinitarian communion" (no. 218). That applies in a very basic way to the church as institution.

Yet, we must recognize that the spirit of communion—and hence the trinitarian root of the church—has been best preserved and lived in religious life and in popular Christianity where power is more shared and a brotherly and sisterly spirit is prominent. It ought to open more and more room for everyone to participate equally, without any discrimination by sex or by the specific function that someone occupies within the church as a whole. Only then will the words of Vatican II ring true: "Thus, the Church shines forth as 'a people made one with the unity of the Father, the Son, and the Holy Spirit'" (*Lumen Gentium*, no. 4).

We likewise observe in social processes today an immense desire for participation, democratization, and change, aiming at forging a more egalitarian, participatory, pluralistic, and family-spirited society. This yearning is in tune with a trinitarian understanding of God. Indeed, it finds in Christian faith in God as communion of the three divine Persons the transcendent utopia of all human strivings for forms that are more participatory, communal, and respecting of diversity. What exists is the Trinity-God. But our emerging situation is making faith in God-Trinity-of-different-Persons all the more relevant. The Trinity is also coming to the fore in political terms. Faith in trinitarian communion can be transformed into a banner of full liberation and a principle for advancing strivings for personal, social, and historic liberation.

---

[1] The 1979 meeting of the Latin American bishops—EDS.

Our reflections here seek to strengthen this social project from the specific field of trinitarian theology. We seek transformations in social relations because we believe in God, Trinity of Persons, in eternal interrelationship and infinite perichoresis. We seek a society that will be more an image and likeness of the Trinity, that will better reflect on the earth the trinitarian communion of heaven, and that will make it easier for us to know the mystery of communion of the divine Three.

This book translates into a more comprehensible language what we have presented in technical terminology in *Trinity and Society* (Orbis Books, 1988). We regard the trinitarian conception of God as so revolutionary for society, the church, and one's own self-understanding as a person, that we have sought to communicate it here in a way that is more aimed at ordinary people, and I hope, more broadly accessible. Because we are dealing with the All-Important and Most Fascinating, we have had to engage in an unending struggle with words, seeking to make them more adequate. Indeed, they fall apart when confronted with the Ineffable of the three divine Persons in community. They become little more than hints and weak arrows pointing toward the mystery that is ever known and yet ever unknown in all human knowing. But we are convinced that they point in the right direction.

Introduction

Holy Trinity, Our Liberation Program

Why get concerned today with the Blessed Trinity? It has been hard enough to believe in a single God. Believing in three Persons who are one God is much harder still! Is believing in God worthwhile? What do we gain by it? What changes in people's lives when they say with all sincerity, "I believe in God; I believe in the Father, in the Son, and in the Holy Spirit, ever together and in a communion of life and love"?

We are convinced that believing in God is worthwhile. We thereby want to express the conviction that it is not death that has the last word but life; it is not the absurd but the full meaning in life that wins the day. To say "I believe in God" means that there is Someone who surrounds me, embraces me everywhere, and loves me, Someone who knows me better than I do myself, deep down in my heart, where not even my beloved can reach, Someone who knows the secret of all mysteries and where all roads lead. I am not alone in this open universe with all my questions for which no one offers me a satisfactory answer. That Someone is with me, and exists for me, and I exist for that Someone and in that Someone's presence. Believing in God means saying: there exists an ultimate tenderness, an ultimate bosom, an infinite womb, in which I can take refuge and finally have peace in the serenity of love. If that is so, believing in God is worthwhile; it makes us more ourselves and empowers our humanity.

But accepting God's existence isn't enough. How does God live? What is God like? This is where the Blessed Trinity comes in. We believe that God is communion rather than solitude. It is not a "one" that is primary but the "three." The three comes first. Then, because of the intimate relationship between the "three" comes the "one" as expressing the unity of the three. Believing in the Trinity means that at the root of everything that exists and subsists there is movement; there is an eternal process of life, of outward movement, of love. Believing in the Trinity means that truth is on the side of communion rather than exclusion; consensus translates truth better than imposition; the participation of many is better than the dictate of a single one. Believing in the Trinity means accepting that everything is related to everything and so makes up one great whole, and that unity comes from a thousand convergences rather than from one factor alone.

We never simply live, we always *live together*. Whatever favors shared life is good and worthwhile. Hence, it is worthwhile believing in this community style of God's existence, of God's trinitarian manner that is always communion and union of three.

We do not need to answer the question, How does this Trinity-God relate to human beings? The answer is obvious: This God includes all and permeates us with its communion. But how does this God relate to the utopia of the poor and the oppressed? They are almost always defeated and convinced by the powerful that they are weak and that they cannot win. But despite everything, dreaming and lying awake, they bear the dream of a humankind without oppressors and oppressed. The oppressed are the true bearers of hope, because they are the only ones who live on hope and need it to keep going, and to stand firm, and to seek liberation. Ultimately, what do the poor want? They want more than just bread, a house, and a job. They want a society organized in such a way that all can earn their bread with their labor and build their house. Such a society will only arise if it is built on the participation of the largest possible number of its members, only if it takes steps to overcome social inequalities, only when it proposes to respect differences and decides to bring about communion among all and with the transcendent Destiny of history.

The Trinity becomes all the more relevant in the context of this striving. In it we find our program of liberation achieved to the infinite: difference and distinction, equality and perfect communion, and union of persons to the point of being a single dynamic, divine reality in eternal reproduction. Looking at the Trinity, we draw conclusions for our own social reality with a view to changing it. Considering our yearnings, particularly those of the oppressed, we discover in the Trinity their utopian embodiment, their ultimate convergence beyond our own imagination.

Believing in the Trinity and in a Communion-God is worthwhile, because such a God is composed of what is most excellent in our nature and is not opposed to our most fundamental strivings. Quite the contrary, such a God comes out to meet us as the full realization of those strivings.

ॐ **I** *ॐ*

In the beginning
is the communion of the Three
not the solitude of a One

1. *From the solitude of a One to the communion of the Three*

What is the God of our faith like? Many Christians imagine God as an infinite Being, almighty, creator of heaven and earth, living alone in heaven with all creation at his feet. He is a kind but solitary God. Others think of him as a merciful father or a harsh judge. But they always think that God is a supreme Being, unique, without possible competitors, in the splendor of his own glory. He may be there with saints, male and female, and angels in heaven. But these are all creatures. As wonderful as they are, they have certainly come from God's hands; they are therefore inferior, only similar to God. God is fundamentally alone, because there is only one God. That is the faith of the Old Testament, of Jews, Muslims, and generally of Christians.

We need to move from the solitude of the One to the communion of the divine Three—Father, Son, and Holy Spirit. In the beginning is communion among several, wealth of diversity, union as expression of the surrender of one divine Person to the other.

If God means three divine Persons in eternal communion among themselves, then we must conclude that we also, sons and daughters, are called to communion. We are image and likeness of the Trinity. Hence, we are community beings. Solitude is hell. No one is an island. We are surrounded by persons, things, and beings on all sides. Because of the Blessed Trinity, we are called to maintain relationships of communion with all, giving and receiving, and together building a rich and open shared life, one that respects differences and does good to all.

Christian faith does not deny the assertion that there is only one God, but it understands God's unity differently. According to New Testament revelation, what actually exists is the Father, the Son, and the Holy Spirit. God is Trinity; God is communion of the divine Three. The Father, the Son, and the Holy Spirit so love one another and are so commingled one with another that they are ever united. What exists is the union of the three divine Persons. The union is so deep and radical that they are a single God. It is like three springs constituting one and the same lake. Each spring runs toward the other; it surrenders all its water to make up a single lake. Or it is like three bulbs in a lamp constituting a single light.

> *Our understanding of God must become Christian. God is always the communion of the three divine Persons. God the Father is never without God the Son and God the Holy Spirit. Confessing that Jesus is God is not enough. It has to be said that Jesus is the God-the-Son of the Father, along with the Holy Spirit. We cannot speak of one Person without speaking of the other two as well.*

∽

2. In the beginning is communion

God is Father, Son, and Holy Spirit in reciprocal communion. They coexist from all eternity; none is before or after, or superior or inferior, to the other. Each Person enwraps the others; all permeate one another and live in one another. This is the reality of trinitarian communion, so infinite and deep that the divine Three are united and are therefore one sole God. The divine unity is communitarian because each Person is in communion with the other two.

What does it mean to say that God is communion and therefore Trinity? Only persons can be in communion. It means that one is in the presence of the other, different from the other but open in a radical mutuality. For there to be true communion there must be direct and immediate relationships: eye to eye, face to face, heart-to-heart. The result of mutual surrender and reciprocal communion is community. Community results from personal relationships in which each is accepted as he or she is, each opens to the other and gives the best of himself or herself.

So to say that God is communion means that the three Eternal Ones, Father, Son and Holy Spirit, are turned toward one another. Each divine Person goes out of self and surrenders to the other two, giving life, love, wisdom, goodness, and everything possessed. The Persons are distinct (the Father is not the Son and the Holy Spirit and so forth) not in order to be separated but to come together and to be able to give themselves to one another.

In the beginning is not the solitude of a One, of an eternal Being, alone and infinite. Rather, in the beginning is the communion of the three Unique Ones. Community is the deepest and most foundational reality that exists. It is because of community that love, friendship, benevolence, and giving exist between human and divine persons. The communion of the Blessed Trinity is not closed in on itself; it opens outward. All creation means an overflow of life and communion of the three divine Persons, inviting all creatures, especially human creatures, to also enter into the play of communion between themselves and with the divine Persons. Jesus himself has said: "That they may all be one. As you, Father, are in me and I am in you, may they also be *in us*" (Jn 17:21).

> *"It has been said beautifully and profoundly, that our God in his most inner mystery is not solitude, but a family. For internally God bears fatherhood, sonship, and the essence of family, which is love. This love, in the divine family, is the Holy Spirit"* (John Paul II at Puebla, on January 28, 1979, speaking to the CELAM Assembly).

ℭℓℐ

3. Why only three divine Persons? Why not two or just one?

There are many people who are intrigued with the number three of the Trinity, for we say that God is Father, is Son, and is Holy Spirit, and hence three divine Persons. The difficulty is compounded when we say the three are one; that is, the *three* Persons are only *one* God. What kind of mathematics is this where three absurdly equals one? Due to such reasoning, they cease believing in the Trinity and give up the core of what is most wonderful in Christianity. Or they say that the proper thing would be to admit three gods or to stay with one sole God.

To begin with, the Trinity (the Father, the Son, and the Holy Spirit) is not about numbers. We are not dealing with mathematics where we add, subtract, divide, or multiply. We are in another realm of thought. When we say "Trinity," we do not intend to do addition—$1 + 1 + 1 = 3$. The very word *Trinity* is a creation of our language; it is not found in the Bible. It began to be used around 150 C.E.; Theodotus, a heretic, used it first, and it was then taken up by the lay theologian Tertullian (d. 220). There is no number in God. When we speak of Father, Son, and Holy Spirit, we are always referring to a Unique One—the Unique One is the denial of all number. The Unique One means there is only one exemplar, as if in the firmament there were only one star, or only one fish in the water, or only one human being on earth, and nothing more. So we must think like this: There only exists the Father as Father and no one else; there only exists the Son as Son and no one else; there only exists the Holy Spirit as Holy Spirit and no one else. Strictly speaking we should not say "three Unique Ones," but each time, the "Unique One" is unique, thus the Father, thus the Son, and thus the Holy Spirit. But to make it easier for us to speak we say— imprecisely—"three Unique Ones," and so "Trinity."

But we cannot stop with such thinking, or we would be right to say, "So there are three gods, because there is the Unique One times three!" We would then find ourselves in tritheism. At this point we must introduce the other truth, *interrelationship*, the inclusion of each Person, *perichoresis*. The Unique Ones are not simply turned in on themselves; they are eternally related to one another. The Father is ever the Father of the Son and of the Holy Spirit. The Son is ever the Son of the Father together with the Holy Spirit. The Holy Spirit is eternally the Spirit of the Son and of the Father. This interaction and harmonization between each Unique One means that there is only God-communion-union.

And it is good that this is how things are: three Persons and only one love, three Unique Ones and only one communion.

If there were only one Unique One, only one God, solitude would ultimately be all there was. Underlying the whole universe, so diverse and so harmonious, would not be communion but only solitude. Everything would end, like the point on a pyramid, at a single, solitary point.

If there were two Unique Ones, the Father and the Son, separation would be uppermost. One would be different from the other; and so there would be exclusion; one would not be the other. There would be no communion between them, and hence no union between Father and Son.

So, with the union and inclusion of the Trinity we reach perfection. Through the Trinity, the solitude of the One is avoided, the separation of the Two (Father and Son) is also overcome, and the exclusion of one from the other (Father from Son, Son from Father) is overcome. The Trinity allows for communion and inclusion. The third Figure reveals the opening and the union of opposites. Hence, the Holy Spirit, the third divine Person, has always been understood as union and communion between Father and Son, inasmuch as that Person is the expression of the flow of life and interpenetration that thrives between the divine Unique Ones for all eternity.

Hence it is not arbitrary that God is communion of three Unique Ones. The Trinity shows that underlying everything existing and moving there dwells an impulse of unification, communion, and eternal synthesis of those who are distinct in an infinite, living, personal, loving, and absolutely fulfilling whole.

Why deny people the true information, that fundamental right of all to know where they have come from, where they are going, and who their true family is? We come from the Trinity, from the heart of the Father, the intelligence of the Son, and the love of the Holy Spirit. We are journeying in pilgrimage toward the reign of the Trinity, which is total communion and eternal life.

⌘

4. It's dangerous to say: One God in heaven and one head on earth

Sticking only with faith in one sole God, without thinking of the Blessed Trinity as the union of Father, Son, and Holy Spirit, is dangerous for society, for political life, and for the church. Saying that God is always the communion of the three divine Persons, however, makes it possible to encourage collaboration, good relationship, and union among the various members of a family, of a community, and of a church. Let us examine the dangers of a rigid monotheism (affirmation of a single God) when not understood as Trinity. It can lead to and justify totalitarianism in politics, authoritarianism in religion, paternalism in society, and machismo in the family.

1. *Totalitarianism in politics.* Some people used to say that just as there is one God in heaven, there must also be one head on earth, thereby giving rise to kings, political leaders, and chiefs who dominated their people with the claim that they were imitating God in heaven. God alone governs and directs the world, without explaining anything to anyone. Political totalitarianism has created arrogance among leaders and submission among the led. Dictators claim to know what is best for the people. They want to exercise freedom; everyone else must accept their orders and obey. Most countries are heirs to such an understanding of power. It has been

thrust into people's heads. That is why it is hard to accept democracy in which everyone exercises freedom and all are children of God.

2. *Authoritarianism in religion.* There are also those who say that just as there is only one God, there is only one Christ, so there ought to be only one religion and one religious head. In keeping with this understanding, the religious community is organized around a single center of power who knows everything, says everything, does everything; all the rest are simple believers, who must abide by what the head decides. Yet that is not how things are understood in the gospels; it is always the community that we see there, and within it are those who serve as coordinators to encourage all.

3. *Paternalism in society.* Some imagine God as a great father. He arranges everything and holds all power for himself. The great lords of this world dominate by invoking in society and in the family the name of God as "boss" or "owner." They forget that God has a Son and lives with the Holy Spirit in perfect equality. God the Father does not replace the efforts of the sons and daughters but indeed invites us to collaborate. Only faith in God-community and communion helps create a family-spirited common life.

4. *Machismo in the family.* As Father, God is represented as being male. The male then assumes all values, downgrading the female. That is how male domination arises in a macho-oriented culture. This culture has hardened all relationships and has kept people from expressing their tenderness, particularly toward women, who are relegated to simply serving men. God is a Father who generates; in revelation God has displayed female and maternal traits. Hence, God is understood also as Mother of boundless goodness. By always thinking of the three, Father, Son, and Holy Spirit, as equals and having the same dignity, we remove the ideological prop for the machismo that is so harmful to our family relationships.

Faith in the Blessed Trinity is a corrective to our deviations and a powerful inspiration for living rightly in the world and in the churches.

If God is Trinity of Persons, community of Father, Son and Holy Spirit, then the creative principle sustaining the unity of all groups, in society and in the churches, ought to be communion among all participants, that is, loving convergence and brotherly and sisterly consensus.

∾

5. A disintegrated experience of the blessed Trinity

Father, Son, and Holy Spirit are always together: they create together, save together, and together they bring us into their communion of life and love. Nothing is done in the Blessed Trinity without the communion of the three Persons. The devotion of many believers reflects a breakdown of the experience of the triune God. Some are left only with the Father, others only with the Son, and finally others only with the Holy Spirit, leading to deviations in our encounter with God that harm the community itself.

1. *Religion of the Father alone.* The father figure is central in the family and in traditional society—he directs, decides, and knows. Thus, some represent God as an almighty Father; judge over life and death, over sons and daughters. We are all dependent on him, and so we are regarded as minors. Such an understanding can lead Christians to feel resigned to their misery and to nourish a spirit of submission to those in charge, to the pope and the bishops, with no creativity. God is certainly Father, but Father of the Son, who, together with the Holy Spirit, live in communion and equality.

2. *Religion of the Son alone.* Others just stand by the figure of the Son, Jesus Christ. He is the companion, the master, or the leader. Among young people, in the Cursillo movement in particular, there has developed an enthusiastic and young image of Christ, brother of all and fiery leader of men and women. This is a Jesus who has relationships only with those alongside of him, without any vertical dimension toward the Father. Such religion creates Christians who lose contact with the people and with the journey of the communities.

3. *Religion of the Holy Spirit alone.* Some groups of Christians are utterly focused on the figure of the Holy Spirit. They cultivate the spirit of prayer, speak in tongues, impose hands, and give vent to their internal and personal emotions. Such Christians forget that the Spirit is always the Spirit of the Son, sent by the Father to continue the liberating work of Jesus. It is not enough to have a relationship that is internal (Holy Spirit), or alongside us (Son), or solely vertical (Father). The three must be integrated. Where would we be if we didn't have the Father to shelter us? Where would we be if this Father hadn't given us his Son to make us children as well? Where would we be if we had not received the Holy Spirit, sent by the Father at the appeal of the Son, to live within us and complete our salvation? Let us live a complete faith in a complete experience of the complete image of God as Trinity of Persons!

> *The human person, to be fully human, needs to be related in three directions: upward, toward the sides, and inwardly. That is how the Trinity comes to meet us: the Father is the infinite "upward," and the Son is the radical "alongside," and the Spirit is the total "within."*

6. *The same glory to the Father, to the Son, and to the Holy Spirit*

A Christian begins and ends the day by praying the "Glory be"—to the Father, to the Son, and to the Holy Spirit. This is much more than a profession of faith in the Christian God, which is ever the triune God; it is praise to the three divine Persons for having revealed themselves in history and having invited us to share in their divine communion. The human response to the revelation of the Blessed Trinity is to give thanks and to glorify. First, we are filled with enthusiasm, because we see that with the existence of the three divine Persons we are surrounded by the life and the love that radiate from their inner communion. Later, we begin to consider how the three Persons are in communion, which qualities each one possesses, and how they relate to creation.

Jesus has revealed to us his secret as a Son and his intimate relationship with the Father in a prayer charged with joy in the Spirit: "I thank you, Father, Lord of heaven and earth. . . . No one knows who the Son is except the Father, or who the Father is except the Son and anyone to whom the Son chooses to reveal him" (Lk 10:21-22). Thus we too approach the Blessed Trinity through prayer, adoration, and thanksgiving.

What are we saying when we pray "Glory be"? Glory in itself is the manifestation of the Trinity just as it is: communion of the divine Three. Glory means revealing the presence of the triune God in history. That presence always brings joy, fascination, and the sense of communion. Knowing that God is communion of three Persons who love one another infinitely and eternally means discovering God's beauty, splendor, and joy. One God alone is without beauty and humor. Three Persons united in communion and in the same life, eternally committed to one another, dazzle us, and produce inner joy. This joy is all the greater when we feel called to participation.

When we pray the "Glory be" we seek to return the glory that we have discovered from God. Glory is paid with glory. We give thanks that the Blessed Trinity wished to be made manifest and to come to dwell with us. We thank the Father for having an only-begotten Son and for creating us sons and daughters in the Son in the power of the Holy Spirit's love. We are happy that God has sent his very Son to be our brother and savior. We rejoice because Father and Son have bestowed on us the Holy Spirit, who helps us accept Jesus Christ and teaches us to pray by saying "Our Father," sanctifying us and drawing us into trinitarian communion, out of our own heart now made temple of the Spirit.

How often while lying in bed at night have I not asked: What is God like, what name expresses the communion of the divine Three? And I have not found any word nor has any light come to me. I've then begun to praise and give glory. That was when my heart became filled with light. I asked no more—I was within the divine communion itself.

∽

7. The blessed Trinity is a mystery ever to be known anew

We commonly say that the Blessed Trinity is the greatest mystery of our faith. How can the three Persons be only one God? Indeed, the Blessed Trinity is an august mystery toward which silence is more appropriate than speech. But we must understand correctly what we mean when we speak of mystery. Normally, mystery is understood to mean a truth revealed by God that cannot be known by human reason: its existence is not known, nor is its content known after its existence has been revealed.

In this sense mystery expresses the bounds of human reason. It seeks to understand, but when it exhausts its forces, it ceases to think and humbly accepts the revealed truth on the basis of divine authority. This idea of mystery was taken on at a time in history when philosophers were seeking to replace divine revelation with philosophy: during the nineteenth century some thinkers went so far as to say that all the truths of Christianity were nothing but natural truths, and hence that they could dispense with the churches and could assimilate the so-called revealed truths into their systems of thought.

The most original and proper understanding of mystery comes from the ancient church. *Mystery* did not mean a reality that was hidden and incomprehensible to the human intellect; rather, *mystery* was God's plan revealed to privileged persons like the great mystics, holy persons, prophets, and apostles, and communicated to everyone else through them. Mystery must be known and recognized by men and women. It does not mean the bounds of reason, but the boundlessness of reason. The more we know God and God's design for communion with human beings, the more we are challenged to know and delve deeper.

Indeed, we can delve more deeply for all eternity without ever reaching the end. We go from one level of knowledge to another, forever expanding the horizons into the infinite of divine life without ever sighting a limit. God is thus life, love, and overwhelming communication, into which we ourselves are plunged. This vision of mystery does not cause anguish but expands our heart. The Blessed Trinity is mystery now and will be for all eternity. We will get to know it more and more, without ever exhausting our desire to know and to be delighted with the knowledge that we are gradually acquiring. We know in order to sing, we sing in order to love, and we love in order to be joined in communion with the divine Persons—Father, Son, and Holy Spirit.

> "God can be that which we cannot understand" (St. Hilary). "O the depth of the riches and wisdom and knowledge of God! How unsearchable are his judgments and how inscrutable his ways! . . . For from him and through him and to him are all things. To him be the glory forever. Amen" (Rom 11:33, 36).

∽

8. Perichoresis: The interpenetration of the three divine Persons

Whenever we speak of the Blessed Trinity we must think of the communion of the divine three—Father, Son, and Holy Spirit. This communion means the union of Persons and accordingly the manifestation of the single triune God. How does this communion among the three divine Persons take place? Orthodox theologians have coined a word that began to spread in the seventh century, especially as used by St. John Damascene (d. 750): *perichoresis*. Since there is no good translation into Portuguese or English or any other language, we opt to keep it in Greek. But we should understand it well, because it opens up for us a fruitful understanding of the Blessed Trinity. First of all, perichoresis means one Person's action of involvement with the other two. Each divine Person permeates the other and allows itself to be permeated by that person. This interpenetration expresses the love and life that constitutes the divine nature. It is the very nature of love to be self-communicating; life naturally expands and seeks to multiply itself. Thus, the divine Three from all eternity find themselves in an infinite explosion of love and life from one to the other.

The effect of this reciprocal interpenetration is that each Person dwells in the other. This is the second meaning of *perichoresis*. In simple words it means that the Father is ever in the Son, communicating life and love to him. The Son is ever in the Father knowing him and lovingly acknowledging him as Father. Father and Son are in the Holy Spirit as mutual expression of life and love. The Holy Spirit is in the Son and the Father as source and manifestation of life and love of this boundless source. All are in all. The Council of Florence defined it well in 1441: "The Father is wholly in the Son and wholly in the Holy Spirit; the Son wholly in the Father and wholly in the Holy Spirit; the Holy Spirit is wholly in the Father and wholly in the Son. None precedes the other in eternity, none exceeds the other in greatness or excels the other in power."

The Blessed Trinity is thus a mystery of inclusion. Such inclusion prevents us from understanding one Person without the others. The Father must always be understood together with the Son and the Holy Spirit and so forth. Someone might think: So there are three gods, the Father, the Son, and the Holy Spirit? There would be, if one were alongside, and unrelated to, the others; there would be, except for the relating and inclusion of the three divine Persons. The Three do not first exist and then relate. Without beginning, they live together eternally and are interconnected. That is why they are one God, God-Trinity.

"In the new world-view, the universe is seen as a dynamic web of interrelated events. . . . All natural phenomena are

ultimately interconnected, and in order to explain any one of them we need to understand all the others. . . . In that sense, one might say that every part 'contains' all the others, and indeed, a vision of mutual embodiment seems to be characteristic of the mystical experience of nature" (Fritjof Capra, The Tao of Physics).

∽

9. The Father's two hands, the Son and the Holy Spirit

How has the Blessed Trinity been revealed? There are two routes that we must follow. First, the Blessed Trinity has been revealed in people's lives, in religions, in history, and then in the life, passion, death, and resurrection of Jesus, and through the manifestation of the Holy Spirit in the communities of the early church and in the process of history down to our own time. Even if men and women knew nothing of the Blessed Trinity, the Father, the Son, and the Holy Spirit always dwelled in people's lives. Whenever people followed the calls of their conscience, whenever they obeyed the light more than the illusions of the flesh, whenever they practiced justice and love in human relations, the Blessed Trinity was present. For the triune God is not found outside these values just mentioned. St. Irenaeus (d. c. 200) put it well: The Son and the Holy Spirit constitute the two hands by which the Father touches us, embraces us, and shapes us ever more in his image and likeness. Son and Holy Spirit have been sent into the world to dwell among us and to bring us into trinitarian communion.

In this sense the Blessed Trinity has ever been present in history, in people's lives and struggles whenever they have lived. We must always distinguish between the reality of the Blessed Trinity and doctrine about it. The reality of the three divine Persons has always accompanied human history. Doctrine arose later when people grasped the revelation of the Blessed Trinity and were able to formulate trinitarian doctrines.

The specific revelation of the Blessed Trinity with all clarity came only through Christ and through the manifestations of the Holy Spirit. Until then, in the religions, in the Hebrew prophets, and in some wisdom texts there appeared only hints of the Trinity. With Jesus there has broken out the clear awareness that God is Father and sends his only-begotten Son, incarnate in Jesus of Nazareth, in the power of the Holy Spirit, who has formed the sacred humanity of Jesus in the womb of the Virgin Mary and filled Jesus with enthusiasm to preach and to heal, and the apostles to bear witness and found Christian communities. We will be able to understand Jesus Christ only if we understand him as the gospels present him to us: as Son of the Father and filled with the Holy Spirit. The Trinity is not revealed as a doctrine but as a practice: in the deeds and words of Jesus and in the action of the Holy Spirit in the world and in people.

Father, stretch out your hand and save us from this misery! And the Father, who hears the cry of his oppressed sons and daughters, has extended his two hands to free us and draw us to his kind bosom: the Son and the Holy Spirit.

∽

❧ **II** ❧

The revealing of the Trinity

10. How has the Father of infinite kindness been revealed?

The most important text presented for the revelation of the Blessed Trinity by Jesus are his parting words in Matthew: "Go therefore and make disciples of all nations, baptizing them in the name of the Father and of the Son and of the Holy Spirit" (28:19). This command of Jesus is found only in Matthew's gospel, not in any of the other three gospels.

Scholars are of the opinion that this formula is late, because it takes into account the baptism experience of the early community during the period when Matthew's gospel was written, around the year 85 C.E. The community had pondered Jesus' words and deeds a great deal, and so it understood that Jesus had indeed revealed who God is, that is, the Blessed Trinity, and that believers should be baptized in the name of that triune God. Jesus is at the origin of that church formula.

Let us consider how Jesus has revealed to us the three divine Persons. Let us begin with the name of the Father. We know that Jesus always calls God *Abba*, an intimate word,

18

something like Daddy. If he thus speaks of God as Father, he is indicating that he feels he is a Son. This Father is infinitely kind and merciful. In long prayers Jesus enjoys deep intimacy with the Father. If he shows himself merciful to sinners, it is because he is imitating the heavenly Father, who is fundamentally merciful and loves the ungrateful and wicked (Lk 6:35).

How does the Father act? The Father acts in the world in order to establish his reign. Jesus makes the message of the reign of God the center of his preaching. *Reign* does not mean a territory over which the king has dominion. Reign is the Father's way of acting by which he continually liberates creation from evil, sin, disease, division, and death, and establishes love, kinship, and life.

With his word and his practice Jesus strives to set up the reign of the Father in this world. He does so, as we shall soon see, in the power of the Holy Spirit. Jesus feels so united to this Father that he can only confess: "The Father and I are one" (Jn 10:30). The Father loved the Son "before the foundation of the world" (Jn 17:24). Therefore even before being Creator, God was and is Father of the eternal Son, who became incarnate and was called Jesus Christ. He reveals the Father because he has said: "Whoever has seen me has seen the Father" (Jn 14:9).

The Father is Father, but not primarily because he is Creator; he was already Father before creation, because he was Father of the Son eternally. In the Son, the Father imagined us as his sons and daughters, and therefore as brothers and sisters of the Son. We have always been in the Father's heart. That is where our roots lie.

৩৯

11. How has the Son, our brother, been revealed?

The Son has been revealed by assuming the sacred humanity of Jesus of Nazareth. But we must respect the path that he chose to reveal himself to people. He did not begin by first saying that he was incarnate in Jesus. Seeing how he prayed, how he acted, and how he spoke, the disciples gradually discovered the reality of Jesus' divine sonship and thus the presence of the second Person of the Blessed Trinity.

First, the Son is revealed in the way that Jesus prayed. He calls God *Abba*. As one who calls God *Abba*, Jesus feels that he is his beloved Son. Indeed, Jesus says, "No one knows the Father except the Son and anyone to whom the Son chooses to reveal him" (Mt 11:27). In praying, Jesus revealed his union and intimacy with the Father; he could say, "The Father and I are one" (Jn 10:30). He felt he was Son, but with the same nature as the Father, experiencing the same communion.

Second, Jesus acted as one who was God's Son and the Father's representative. He had compassion on all who were suffering and poor. He healed and consoled. Those who were helped felt they were standing before God's power in person. Peter was right to exclaim, "You are the Son of the living God!" Jesus' enemies realized that Jesus was moving into the divine domain. He forgave sins, something only God can do, and he modified the old law or introduced liberating interpretations. They were right when they claimed that he had "made himself equal to God" (Jn 5:18).

Third, heaven itself gave witness on behalf of Jesus, the Son of God. We do not know whether the biblical account refers to a specific event or whether this is a literary way of expressing the inner experience of Jesus, communicated in

some manner to the disciples. In all such instances, at Jesus'
baptism and at the transfiguration on Mount Tabor, a voice
was heard, "This is my Son, the Beloved, with whom I am
well pleased" (Mt 3:17; cf. 17:5).

Finally, the death and resurrection of Jesus are crucial
moments in which the true nature of God and of the other
two divine Persons is revealed: love and full communion. In
death, Jesus totally surrenders his life to others. This death
results from the rejection that Jesus has suffered. But he does
not allow death to be simply the expression of rejection of
him, and of the God he proclaims, and of the reign. He freely
assumes death as ultimate expression of his love for whoever
rejects him. He wants the last word to be that of communion rather than exclusion. Jesus dies in solidarity and in communion even with the enemies who condemn him so as to
assure the victory of love and communion. This victory is
revealed in the resurrection, which is the fullness of life in
total communication and fulfillment. This life revealed in
the resurrection is the same one that was on the cross. Hence,
there is a vital unity between death and resurrection; there
is a single paschal mystery. This mystery reveals the essence
of the Blessed Trinity: love and communion. Present in this
mystery is the Father, who loves and suffers with the Son,
and the Holy Spirit through whose power the Son surrenders his life and maintains communion to the end.

*If we want to be united with the Blessed Trinity, we must
follow the same path as Jesus: pray with intimacy, act radically on behalf of justice and communion, and accept our
own death as a kind of total surrender and ultimate communion even with our enemies.*

☙

12. How has the Holy Spirit, our strength, been revealed?

The Holy Spirit is the second hand by which the Father reaches out to us and embraces us. Father and Son have sent the Holy Spirit into the world. First, the Spirit is ever acting on earth, motivating life, bolstering the courage of the prophets, and inspiring wisdom for human actions. The Spirit's great work has been to come down upon Mary to form in her womb the sacred humanity of the Son incarnate in Jesus; the Spirit descended upon Jesus when he was baptized by John; in the strength of the Spirit, Christ performs signs that liberate from human ills. Jesus himself says, "If it is by the Spirit of God that I cast out demons, then the kingdom of God has come to you" (Mt 12:28). After the ascension of Jesus into heaven, it is the Spirit who deepens and spreads Christ's message, brings us to accept with faith and love the Person of the Son, and teaches us to pray: Abba, our Father!

The revelation of the Spirit takes place in four privileged places. The first is the Virgin Mary. The Spirit dwelled in her and raised her to the height of the divine. Hence he who is born of Mary, as St. Luke says, shall be called Son of God (Lk 1:35). The feminine has been touched by the Divine and also made eternal. Woman has her place in God.

The second place is Christ. He was filled with the Spirit. Hence, he was the new human, fully free, and liberated from the age-old bonds. In the power of the Spirit, he launches his messianic program of complete liberation (Lk 4:18-21). The Spirit and Christ will ever be united to lead creation back to the bosom of the Blessed Trinity.

The third place is mission. The Spirit descends upon the apostles at Pentecost, removes their fear, and sends them to spread Christ's message among all peoples. It is the Spirit who in mission makes it possible to see and achieve unity amid the variety of nations and languages. Variety need not mean confusion but can mean the wealth of unity.

The fourth place is human and church community. In human community many services and capabilities come to the fore. Some people are able to console, others to coordinate, others to write, still others to build. Likewise in the Christian community there exists every kind of service and ministry, whether for the good of the community or the good of society, often breaking patterns and starting something new. Everything comes from the Spirit. Christians have meditated on all these manifestations and have concluded that the Spirit is also God, together with the Father and the Son. They are not three gods, but one God in communion of Persons.

These are the signs of the presence of the Spirit: when there is enthusiasm in the work of the community; when there is courage to devise new approaches to new problems; when there is resistance to all oppression; when there is a will to liberation that begins with justice for the poor; when there is hunger and thirst for God and tender feeling in the heart.

∾

13. The trinitarian awareness of the early Christians

The revelation of the Blessed Trinity is present in the New Testament, but there is no well-elaborated doctrine on it. Doctrine involves questioning, reflection, and systematizing ideas. That kind of thing was to arise only two centuries later, when Christians had to work out clear ideas on the divinity of Jesus and the Holy Spirit.

Yet trinitarian awareness can be seen in the writings of the early Christians, and especially the letters of St. Paul, St. Peter, and St. John. This awareness is expressed in three-fold formulas; that is, ways of thinking and speaking in which the Father, the Son, and the Holy Spirit always appear together. *Faith* in the Blessed Trinity is thus already there, even though no clearly elaborated *doctrine* on the Blessed Trinity can be plainly seen there—or it is just there in embryo. Let us roll out some of the more significant texts.

The first comes from the church community of St. Matthew: "Go therefore and make disciples of all nations, baptizing them in the name of the Father and of the Son and of the Holy Spirit" (28:19). We have already said that this text is late (around 85 C.E.); it means that by baptism the believer is introduced into the communion of the Trinity and is under the protection of the divine Three.

The second such text is the one from Paul, now used in all masses: "The grace of the Lord Jesus Christ, the love of God (Father), and the communion of the Holy Spirit be with all of you" (2 Cor 13:13). The threefold formula is so explicit that it needs no comment.

Another trinitarian text is in the letter to the Thessalonians:

> But we must always give thanks to God for you, brothers and sisters beloved by the Lord, because God chose you as the first fruits for salvation through sanctification by the Spirit and through belief in the truth. For this purpose he called you through our proclamation of the good news, so that you may obtain the glory of our Lord Jesus Christ. (2 Thes 2:13-14)

The divine Three appear here together. It must be kept in mind that whenever the New Testament speaks of God, it is understood to be speaking of the Father. Similar texts are found in 1 Corinthians 12:4-6; Galatians 3:11-14; 2 Corinthians 1:21-22 and 3:3; Romans 14:17-18 and 15:16; Philippians 3:3; Ephesians 2:20-22 and 3:14-16.

We highlight still other texts because they are so clear: "And because you are children, God has sent the Spirit of his Son into our hearts, crying, 'Abba! Father!'" (Gal 4:6). "But it is God who establishes us with you in Christ and has anointed us, by putting his seal on us and giving us his Spirit in our hearts as a first installment" (2 Cor 1:21-22). "For through him [Jesus] both of us have access in one Spirit to the Father" (Eph 2:18). Other texts that could be read without much explanation include Titus 3:4-6, 1 Peter 1:2, Jude 20-21, Revelation 1:4, 5, and still others. The tenor of these texts is always that in the work of God's liberating approach to human beings, the three Divine Ones always emerge in communion, acting together and bringing us into their divine life.

More important than awareness of the good is doing good. More important than knowing how the Father, Son, and Holy Spirit are one God is living the communion that is the essence of the Trinity.

༄

14. The Old Testament preparation for the revelation of the Blessed Trinity

If the only true God is called Trinity of Persons—Father, Son, and Holy Spirit—then we must also admit that all divine revelation at any point of history means a revelation of the Blessed Trinity. Certainly people are not aware that the encounter with God always means an encounter with the three divine Persons, but once this truth is discovered we can always say that every authentic experience of God means a revelation of the Blessed Trinity. We can reread the religions of the world, and the Hebrew scriptures in particular, in the light of this truth. There we recognize signs of an awareness that there is diversity in God and that there is communion and love in God's life. Thus the Hebrew scriptures give voice to the faith that there is only one God, but at the same time they attest that God has gone out of Godself and has established a covenant with men and women, that God takes the side of the oppressed and wills their liberation.

In the Hebrew scriptures we discover three personifications that hint at future faith in the Blessed Trinity. First, Wisdom is personified. She is God present among human beings, opening paths where there are doubts, casting light in the midst of human searching. She is God but is relatively autonomous from God, properly speaking. Second, the Word of God is personified. Through the Word, God is in the midst of the community; through it, he communicates his will, judges history, saves, and promises the Liberator to come. This Word is God but at the same time gains relative independence from God, thereby showing that there is both unity and diversity in God. Finally, the power of God is also personified. It is the Spirit of wisdom, discernment, courage, and holiness. This power of God is manifested in creation, in history, in the lives of people, particularly the righteous and the prophets. The New Testament saw the presence of the Holy Spirit, third Person of the Blessed Trinity, in these manifestations.

The Blessed Trinity has sought to gradually manifest itself to human persons. First, as St. Epiphanius taught: "Unity is taught in Moses; second, duality is proclaimed in the prophets, and third, the Trinity is found in the gospels."

Revelation is like life. What is to come forth is always prepared. Dawn prepares for the rising sun, as the seed does for the plant, and the flower for the fruit. Likewise the Old Testament prepares the New; the God of the covenant prepares the God of communion.

∽ III ∽

Human reason
and the Blessed Trinity

15. How Christians have expressed
the Blessed Trinity

The coming of the Son and the Holy Spirit began a new age for humankind. Seeing Christ's words and actions, and alert to the manifestations of the Holy Spirit, the early Christians drew the conclusion that God the Father had sent the Son and the Holy Spirit and that the three were God in communion and intercommunication.

At first there was no theological reflection on this conviction. It was in the setting of the liturgy that trinitarian faith was first expressed. The *doxologies*—prayers of praise and thanksgiving—offered the earliest opportunities for the faithful to give witness to the presence of the Father, the Son, and the Holy Spirit. The ancient prayers, like ours today, always ended with "Glory be to the Father, through the Son, in the unity of the Holy Spirit."

Then came sacramental practice. Baptism and eucharist were celebrated with solemnity. In keeping with the command of the Risen One preserved in Matthew (28:19), Christians baptized "in the name of the Father, and of the Son, and of the Holy Spirit." The first mass formulas (anaphoras) were always structured in a trinitarian manner. The Father is always the end and objective of every celebration. The mysteries of the life, passion, death, resurrection, and ascension of Jesus are celebrated, while the coming of the Spirit at Pentecost and the Spirit's activity in the community and in history are also recalled. Everything is done to bring people into trinitarian communion.

We are also familiar with the early creeds (called *symbols* in the early church). A clear trinitarian awareness can already be seen in them. The current baptism ritual still preserves the same structure as the second-century expression of faith in Rome, which reads, "I believe in God, Father almighty . . . and in Jesus Christ, his only Son Our Lord. . . . I believe in the Holy Spirit." Even today Christians are accustomed to beginning and ending the day by making the sign of the cross, which is an expression of faith in the Christian God, who is always communion and joint presence of the three Persons.

Finally, theological reflections began in the third century. Reflection was first on the true nature of Christ, which is the same as that of the Father; therefore he is truly God as and with the Father. Then it became clear that the Spirit, who is with the Father and the Son, is therefore God. Only at the Council of Constantinople (381) was it defined in so many words that God is three *Persons* in the unity of a single *nature* of love and communion.

Self-conscious thinking does not have the first word. First comes life, celebration of life, and work—then comes reflection and doctrine. The same thing happened with the first Christians. They began praising the Father, the Son, and the Holy Spirit, then baptizing persons in the name of the Trinity. Only later end did they begin to reflect on what they were celebrating and doing.

⚮

16. *Three ways of understanding the Blessed Trinity*

Throughout history Christians have developed three main approaches to presenting the mystery of the Blessed Trinity more systematically. Where shall we begin? Let us look at these approaches: Greek, Latin, and modern.

The *Greeks* started with the Person of the Father. In him they saw the source and principle of the entire divinity and of everything that exists. The creed says, "I believe in God, the Father almighty." This Father is full of intelligence and love. In expressing himself, he produces out of himself a Son as the supreme expression of his nature, who is his Word revealing his mystery without beginning. In emitting the Word (the Son), he also issues the Breath. He breathes out the Holy Spirit, who comes from the Father simultaneously with the Son. Thus, the Father entrusts to the two Persons all his substance and nature. In this manner the three are consubstantial, that is, together they have the same nature, and hence are God.

The *Latins* started from the single divine nature. This nature is spiritual. Hence it is full of vitality and inner dynamism. This spiritual principle, insofar as it is eternal, without beginning or end, is called Father. Insofar as the Father knows himself, he projects himself outward as Word and produces the Son. Insofar as Father and Son are turned toward one another, recognize one another, and love one another, they together spirate (as from a single principle, as from a single movement) the Holy Spirit. If, in the creed, the Greeks accented the term *Father* ("I believe in God the Father almighty"), the Latins focused more on *God* ("I believe in God"); only later did they go on to the Person of the Father.

Moderns prefer starting with the relationships among the three divine Persons. They definitely start with what is novel in Christianity. God is, from the beginning, Father, Son, and Holy Spirit. But the three Persons are commingled among themselves; they weave among themselves a bond of love so intimate and strong that they are a single God. They are three lovers of a single love or three Subjects of a single communion.

Each of these visions has its advantages. In a world where the tendency is to worship many gods and fetishes, it is a good idea to start from the unity of the divine nature. In a situation where the accent falls too much on the unity and the absoluteness of God and the concentration of political and religious power, it is well to start with the trinity of Persons in communion. In a self-centered society, in which there is not enough communion to humanize relations and differences are not respected, it is well to start with equal, loving, and unifying relations among the three Persons. Thus it can be seen that the Blessed Trinity is perfect communion and that it offers Christians their liberation program.

Philosophers like to talk of God as the Absolute. Such language has a disadvantage: it always sets up a fundamental dualism between the Absolute and the relative, between eternity and time, between God and the world. We Christians prefer to speak of the communion of the divine Persons, which is always inclusive, because it also includes humankind, the world, and time.

☙

17. Key words for expressing faith in the Blessed Trinity

After 150 years of thinking, arguments, and bishops' meetings, the church reached the point of settling on the key words with which its faith in the Blessed Trinity can be expressed without error and without distortion. The expressions admittedly look cold and formal. They must be completed with a heart set aflame by knowing that it is the vessel in which the three divine Persons dwell.

One sole divine nature expresses what unites the Trinity and makes the three persons to be one sole God. The church has used the word *nature* (substance or essence). Nature is God's essence in its dynamic aspect, and hence that which constitutes God as God, different from any other possible being. This nature is numerically one and is present in the Father, the Son, and the Holy Spirit.

Person is that which distinguishes within God, that is, the Father, the Son, and the Holy Spirit. We understand *person* to mean that individuality that exists in itself, turned toward others, in a singular existence different from others. Thus the Father is distinct from the Son, although he is not something other than the Father, for he has the same nature. It is proper to each Person to be open to the others and to surrender totally in such a manner that the Father is fully in the Son and in the Holy Spirit and so for each Person in turn.

Processions designate the manner and the order in which one Person proceeds from the other. There are two processes: the generation of the Son, and the spiration of the Holy Spirit. It is said that the Father knows himself absolutely. This operation is so absolute in the Father that he *generates* the Son. The Father does not cause the Son, but he totally communicates to him his own being. Father and Son contemplate one another and love one another. This love makes both spirate the Holy Spirit as expression of the love of the Father and the Son.

Relations are the connections existing among the three divine Persons. With relation to the Son, the Father has paternity; with relation to the Father, the Son has filiation; with relation to the Holy Spirit, the Father and Son have active spiration; vis-à-vis the Father and the Son, the Holy Spirit has passive spiration. The relations make it possible to distinguish one Person from another. But the Persons are also distinguished by their own Personhood.

Missions designate the presence of the divine Persons within history; thus it is said that the Father, in generating the Son, has planned all of creation; the Son became incarnate to divinize and redeem us; the Holy Spirit has been sent in mission to sanctify us and bring everything back to the reign of the Trinity. With these words we glimpse a little of the divine mystery of communion and infinite love.

> *It is not words that have been revealed to us but Persons—the Father, the Son, and the Holy Spirit. The words only have value when they remind us and bring us to the divine Persons. Hence, they must be used with devotion and love. Otherwise they are like camels who go blind before they reach the oasis of bubbling waters.*

☙

18. Erroneous ways of understanding the Blessed Trinity

From the outset Christian faith has professed that the God revealed by Jesus is Trinity—Father, Son, and Holy Spirit.

At first there were no problems because Christians had not yet felt the need to deepen the implications of their faith. How combine faith in one God, as was believed in the Old Testament, with the New Testament faith, which states that there is a Trinity? In the church of the past and lasting up to our own time there have been three erroneous ways of understanding the Blessed Trinity: modalism, subordinationism, and tritheism. Let us look at each of them.

Modalism is the error according to which the Blessed Trinity represents three modes by which one and the same God appears to human beings. God can only be one and dwells in inaccessible light. Therefore, say the modalists, when God reveals himself to human beings, he appears under three different masks. When it is said that God creates, he appears with the mask of the Father. When God is said to save, he appears under the mask of the Son. When it is said that God sanctifies and brings all of creation back to the reign of heaven, the same one God appears under the form of the Holy Spirit. It is only for us that God is Trinity; in himself he is simply the sole solitary God. This erroneous understanding means giving up the characteristically Christian idea of God as the communion of the three Unique Ones—the Father, the Son, and the Holy Spirit. This way of representing the Blessed Trinity was condemned by the church both in ancient times and subsequently.

Subordinationism means that the Son and the Holy Spirit are subordinated to the Father. Only the Father is fully God. The Son is the highest creature that the Father has created— but he is not God. At most he has a human nature like that of the Father, but he is never equal and with the same nature as the Father. The same is said of the Holy Spirit. He is dependent on the Father and is not God. Others have gone so far as to say that the Son is only adopted but never unbegotten and of the same substance as the Father. This understanding leads to the loss of the equality among the three divine Persons and also the full divinity of each of them. The church condemned this doctrine, especially at the Council of Nicea (325).

Finally, there is *tritheism*. Some Christians said that there are three divine Persons, but they are three gods, distinct and separate from one another. This doctrine was rejected. How can there be three infinite ones? Three absolute ones? Three eternal ones? The three Persons are eternally related and in communion to the point of being a single God-of-love-and-life.

These errors have forced Christians to deepen their knowledge of the Blessed Trinity, ever maintaining the unity of love and the trinity of loving Persons.

Erroneous doctrines are generally one-eyed readings of the truth. To contemplate the truth with both eyes, our reason has to work hard. Erroneous doctrines do not force us to do that. Hence they represent not an absolute disaster but a chance accident along a true path.

ↂ

✑ IV ✑

Human imagination
and the Blessed Trinity

19. Believing also with our imagination

We do not believe with a loving heart and a thinking head alone. We also believe with our imagination. Without imagination we are almost nothing. Our experience is enhanced through imagination and all reality takes on color. We can only learn what God has promised us if we use our imagination, because the human mind barely grasps the present and conjures up God with ideas drawn from the world. Jesus himself, when he describes the kingdom of God for us, uses images: the seed, the hidden treasure, the banquet, the owner who arrives at his farm without warning. Christian thinkers from the earliest centuries have used images to better understand and communicate some idea of the august mystery of the Trinity. Thus, for example, St. Ignatius of Antioch (d. 104) wrote a letter to the Ephesians, in which he speaks of the Blessed Trinity in this manner, "You are stones of the temple of the Father, prepared for the construction of God the Father, raised up on high by the lever of *Jesus Christ*, the lever which is the cross, you using the *Holy Spirit* like a rope."

Here the three divine Persons appear acting in history on behalf of the salvation of the world.

The icon of the Russian Andrei Rublev (c. 1410) is also widely known. It presents the three divine persons in the form of the three angels who appeared to Abraham at Mamre (Gn 18:1-5), and who then disappeared, leaving a clear impression of a visit from God. The three are seated around a table on which is the eucharist. They are equal to one another, and yet they are different. They gaze at one another with respect and in deep loving communion. The eucharist signifies the presence of Christ and together with him that of the Spirit, who has been sent by the Father, that is, the entire Blessed Trinity living with us on earth.

Another very significant representation is found in a small church in Bavaria (Urschalling bei Prien). In it the Holy Spirit is seen in the form of a woman, with the Father on one side and the Son on the other. They are respectfully placing their hands on the Holy Spirit's breasts. At the bottom they are united as though they were a single body, clothed in a long tunic. Again we have unity (the same nature of love and communion). In the Church of the Trinity in Goiás, the Blessed Trinity is also represented crowning Our Lady, who stands for all creation. No wonder Christians there wrote on a large panel, "The Blessed Trinity is perfect community," as a greeting to Christian base communities throughout Brazil.

We are temples of the Blessed Trinity, which is in each and every dimension of us. Every faculty of our spirit is worthy to praise and acknowledge the divine Persons. Is imagination less worthy because it dreams rather than thinks, because it has images rather than ideas? In its way it also blesses the holy Trinity.

☙

20. *The human person as image of the Trinity*

In Genesis the human person is said to be created in the image and likeness of God (Gn 1:27). To us as Christians, this means that each human person, man or woman, reveals traces of the Blessed Trinity—the only truly existing God. How does the image of the Father, the Son, and the Holy Spirit appear in the human being? The theologian who pursued this question most profoundly was St. Augustine, and what he said remains valid to this day.

All human persons, first of all, find that they are a mystery to themselves. As much as we know ourselves, as others know us, and as the sciences provide us with more and more data on human existence, we remain a deep mystery to ourselves. That is why we cannot judge anyone and must maintain a stance of respectful listening toward each human person, no matter how lowly. Each has something to say and to reveal, and with such revelations we can better discover the countenance of the triune God. As an abyss of mystery, the human person represents the Father, who as divine Person, principle without principle, is the primary and fundamental mystery.

As mystery, persons have intelligence and communicate beyond themselves. They know themselves and create an entire world of representations and ideas. They speak their own truth. This truth or word of themselves represents the Son, who is the Father's Truth and revealed Word. Hence, whenever we are thinking properly, whenever we say the truth about ourselves and about the things of the world, we are serving the divine Word revealed in us.

Persons do not simply acknowledge one another; they also love. They wish to be united to other persons and to things.

The Holy Spirit is the love within the Blessed Trinity, who unites Father and Son, bringing it about that the Father-Son opposition is overcome. Through the Spirit there is revealed among the three Persons a union of eternal communion and love ever knitting them together. When we love and feel linked in kinship with others, we are revealing in history what the Holy Spirit means.

The person—as mystery, intelligence, and love—constitutes a dynamic and ever-open unity—these are not three things in juxtaposition. It is always the person who is mystery, who thinks, and who loves. Thus, each of us, in our own unity and diversity, is image and likeness of God, who is Father, Son, and Holy Spirit. Should we not treat each person with the utmost respect, because each one is a temple of the Blessed Trinity?

> *If we violate human nature, if we trample on the rights of the person, if we show contempt for the poor, we destroy all routes giving access to the God-of-life-and-communion. The compass for all journeys is respect for the human person, image of the Trinity. Disrespect destroys the needle, and then there's no compass left.*

∾

21. The human family, symbol of the Trinity

Every human being bears the traces of the three divine Persons in his or her entire being and activity. Every human being is born in a family, where signs of the presence of the triune God can be seen. God is communion and community of Persons—and the family is built on communion and on love. It is the primary expression of human community.

In every complete and traditional family we find three elements: the father, the mother, and the child—a diversity of persons. The father, in our culture, is the expression of love embodied in work, in building the home, and in security. The mother, as we see her, is love generating and protecting life, the intimacy of the home, and sheltering warmth. Father and mother become intertwined in love, in mutual recognition and admiration, in the very endeavor of bringing up their family. They live under the same roof, share the same worries, and commune in the same joys. The expression of this communion and mutual recognition is the child who is born, who unites the two, and turns husband and wife into father and mother. They both go out of themselves and concentrate on something beyond themselves, which is the fruit of the loving relationship between them: the child. In the family we have an image—one of the richest—of the Blessed Trinity. First, there are the three elements: father, mother, child. Then there is the distinction of persons— one is not the other. Each has his or her own autonomy and proper task. Yet they are related by vital bonds like love. There is a single communion of life. And so while remaining three, they make up a single family. The unity of the family is similar to that of the Blessed Trinity. Unity is the expression of love, of each Person's going out to the other, of sharing the same life. Recognition between father and mother is like that between the Father and the Son. The child unites father and mother; analogously, the Holy Spirit, who proceeds from the Father and the Son, unites the Father and the Son. That is why the Holy Spirit is said to be unifying love—the divine Person who unites the eternal Persons and human persons.

In order to be the sacrament of the Trinity, the family must seek its perfection. Throughout history the human family has also been marked by sin and disunity. But whenever the family seeks integration and thoroughly living out love, it becomes a sign of the triune God in history.

In a well-functioning family we find the main dimensions of the Blessed Trinity: distinction (father, mother, children) and union in a single life, a single love, and a shared communion in the interweaving of the three who constitute a single family. We are born into the bosom of a family, and we will live eternally as sons and daughters in the divine Family.

cᴓ

22. Society as image of the Trinity

Human persons do not live solely in themselves, in the depths of their individual mystery, nor are they simply born from a family as an expression of love between husband and wife. A person is part of human society, into which both person and family are set. For one who looks intently, society is a powerful sign of the Blessed Trinity in history.

Society is not something that appears ready-made by either God or nature. Society is the result of three forces that always act together and continually; in these forces we can identify the traces of the Trinity.

First, there is economic power, by which we organize the production and reproduction of human life. By means of the economy we prepare the foods that the body needs. In a socially organized manner we produce, distribute, and consume them. Economic power never has to do solely with material and "economic" matters. We are always dealing with human matters, because eating, making a living, and assuring food for someone who is hungry are profoundly human and hence spiritual. This power underlies all the rest, because without it there is no life. And without life, there is neither society, nor religion, nor adoration.

Second, there is political power, by which we organize ourselves socially, distributing power, professions, and responsibilities. Through politics we create human relations and plan the institutions needed to make society work and to satisfy people's material, spiritual, and cultural needs.

Third, and finally, there is cultural power, by which we create the values and meanings that give validity and expression to our life and what we do. Cultural power gives rise to religious rituals, philosophies, the arts, and all the symbols by which we express our thoughts and values. No one lives without valuing the things he or she does or that are nearby.

These three forces are mingled in the building, establishment, and development of every human society. They always work together, and so the political and the cultural are within the economic, and so forth.

This is just what we say of the Blessed Trinity: the three Persons are distinct, but they always act together. The interrelationship among the divine Three means that they are but one God, mirrored in our social reality.

The communion that is to be fashioned between human beings is one that embraces their whole being, right down to the roots of their love. It must also manifest itself in every aspect of life, including economic, social, and political life. Produced by the Father, the Son, and the Holy Spirit, it is the communication of their own trinitarian communion.

⤶

23. The church, great symbol of the Trinity

A great third-century theologian, Tertullian, one of the first to formulate the doctrine of the Trinity, wrote, "Where the Father, the Son, and the Holy Spirit are, there also is the church, which is the body of the Three." The trinitarian mystery is reflected in each human person, in the family, and in society. But it is in the church that this august mystery of communion and life finds its most visible expression in history.

The church is inherently the community of faith, hope, and love seeking to live the ideal of union proposed by Jesus Christ himself: " . . . that they may all be one. As you, Father, are in me and I am in you, may they also be in us" (Jn 17:21). The unity of Christians lies not in bureaucratic leveling, but in a commingling of the faithful with one another and with their pastors at the service of others.

The church is built along three fundamental lines of force, and that is where its likeness with the divine Three is seen most specifically: it is built on faith; celebration of faith; and organization for the sake of internal cohesion, charity, and mission in the midst of human beings. These three moments are the embodiment of the community that comes together to proclaim and deepen faith, to celebrate the presence of the risen Christ and his spirit in human history and especially in the Christian community itself, and to become organized for solid service to all people, starting with the poor. Faith, celebration, and organization are not independent of one another; they are the church itself in a dynamic movement of life and service. The church's communion is not expressed merely in the religious field. It also takes place in a social project of communion of goods, sharing of life, and creation of kinship, as can be clearly seen in the Acts of the Apostles, which gives an account of the life of the early apostolic community (Acts 2:44-45, 4:34-36).

When Tertullian says that the church is the body of the three divine Persons, he intends to suggest that by the living out of faith, sharing in worship, and the holy organization, something is made known of the mystery of the Father, of the intelligence of the Son, and of the love of the Holy Spirit. The church is all of this, not simply because it is church, but because it lives consistently the gospel message of being a place of ardent faith, unconquerable hope, and committed love in the world.

> The more the church imbibes from its eternal fountain, the trinitarian communion by which the three Distinct Ones are unified and are one God, the more it will overcome its internal divisions. It will cease being clerical and lay, and will become a space of equal relationships in a single people of God, of true brothers and sisters serving the reign of the Trinity.

෴

24. The world, sacrament of the Trinity

All creation is work of the blessed Trinity. The Persons act on the basis of their own proper qualities so that signs of the triune God can be seen everywhere. God in God's own mystery can never be adequately represented. That is why the Fourth Lateran Council (1215) taught that the unlikeness between Creator and creature is greater than the likeness. But that does not mean that we do not have the traces of the divine stamped on all creation.

Scholars such as the renowned psychologist Carl Gustav Jung have studied, for example, the symbolism of the number three. This number is an archetype (a deep template in the soul on the basis of which we grasp our experiences) found in all cultures. It also manifests itself in the unconscious. The number three symbolizes the human demand for integration, association, and totality. Sometimes alongside the Trinity, there comes a fourth element, often in a feminine manner, such as Mary, creation, or Wisdom. This fourth element seeks to express the community of the Three turned outward; they communicate among themselves and invite persons and creation into that communion of love and life that is proper to the life of the Trinity.

In preaching, analogies and figures have been borrowed from material life to express the trinity of Persons and their unity and communion. Thus, some speak of the sun, its ray, and its heat. Others speak of fire that radiates light and produces heat. Still others point to three lit candles that meet in a single flame. Many catechists show children the shamrock, which is a leaf made up of three small leaflets.

Yet others appeal to the three basic forces of the universe: gravity, electromagnetic force, and atomic energy. All three are the expression of the single universal energy. More and more scientists are abandoning the classic vision of elementary particles of matter (proton, neutron, electron) and are postulating that all factors interact in a true cosmic perichoresis; they use the word that theology has also used—*interpenetration* of all with all. These trinitarian relations are reflected in the cosmos. Who has not pondered the equilateral triangle? It has three equal sides, making up a single surface.

Obviously these images are pale, lifeless pointers to the living mystery of the Father, the Son, and the Holy Spirit, distinct in Persons but eternally united in love and communion.

In short, no image or concept can express the depth of trinitarian love. Only the heart, which is greater than our intelligence, can glimpse the greatness and the marvel of the divine life, for by the heart we enter into communion with the divine Persons and share in their inner life.

Nature is not mute; the stones speak, the sea expresses itself, and the firmament sings God's glory. Nothing is juxtaposed or thrown in randomly. Everything is related and enters into communion: the wind with the rock, the rock with the earth, the earth with the sun, and the sun with the universe. Everything is drenched in the communion of the Blessed Trinity.

V

What the Blessed Trinity is: Communion of life and love among the divine Three

25. The Trinity is an eternal communication of life

The Christian God is eternal communion of the divine Three—Father, Son, and Holy Spirit. They are eternally pouring forth, one toward the other, so much so that they build a single movement of love, communication, and encounter. How can we better understand this? It is not a matter of removing the veil from the mystery of God, but rather of grasping the divine movement so that we may better experience the presence and activity of the Blessed Trinity in the world and in our own personal journey. Biblical theology has found a word to express this divine thrust: *life*. God is understood as a living activity that is eternal, life-giving, and protective of all life that is threatened, such as that of the poor and those who suffer injustice. Jesus himself, the incarnate Son, presented himself as one who came to bring life and life in abundance (Jn 10:10). If we briefly consider

47

what life is about, we will better grasp the communion of the divine Three.

Life is a mystery of spontaneity, an inexhaustible process of giving and receiving, assimilating, incorporating, and surrendering one's own life in communion with other life. The phenomenon of life entails expansion and presence. A living being is not present as a stone is present. A living being has presence, which means an intensification of existence. The living being speaks for itself; it does not need words to communicate itself. When faced with a living being, we must take a stance: accept or reject the life of the other. Every life includes a process of communion with something different with which it enters into osmosis, incorporating it into itself. All life is reproduced in another life. Life is by its nature expansive. It always means an open process with new expressions of life. We understand something of the Blessed Trinity if we connect it to the mystery of life. Father, Son, and Holy Spirit are eternal Living Ones, fulfilling themselves insofar as they surrender themselves to one another. The fundamental characteristic of each divine Person is to be for the others, through the others, with the others, and in the others. Each living Person is eternally vivified by vivifying the others and sharing the life of the others. Thus, as a person becomes happy only by making others happy, so it is in the trinitarian life: each Person is alive insofar as it gives life to the others and receives life from the others. Because that is the case, we understand why the Christian God can only be the communion of the divine Three and must be Trinity. It is more than duality, more than the Father face to face with the Son. It is Trinity because it means the inclusion of a Third to express the fullness of life beyond mutual contemplation: the Holy Spirit. Thus life constitutes God's essence, life is communion given and received, and communion is the Trinity.

We do not know what life is, but it involves movement, spontaneity, freedom, future, and newness. The Trinity is eternal life, and so it is freedom, perennial giving and receiving, invention and giving of self without ceasing. The Trinity is newness, as is each life, ever changing but without dispersion. Each Person is future for the others and hence ever new and surprising.

❧

26. I-Thou-We: The Blessed Trinity

The mystery of the Blessed Trinity has always challenged the understanding of theologians, that is, those Christians who devote their lives to thinking about and pursuing the truths that God has revealed to us. The great councils set the primary frameworks, in the light of which we must orient our thinking about the Blessed Trinity. But they have never closed questions. They always recognize the insufficiencies of human language. At the end of all our efforts, we always end up in reverent silence. But before going silent we must speak and employ every intellectual effort to create more and more light, for that is the only way we will do justice to the greatness of God and to the depth of God's mystery. Thus, in recent decades the concept of person as applied to the Father, the Son, and the Holy Spirit has been deepened a great deal. In common teaching *person* used to be understood as individuality existing in itself, distinct from any other. Thus Father, Son, and Holy Spirit are distinct from one another and have a single existence. In modern times this idea has been deepened by accentuating an aspect that was not sufficiently developed in the past, even though it could be found in many Christian theologians. *Person* is indeed a being-in-oneself and hence means irreducible individuality, but this individuality is characterized by the fact of being always open to others. *Person* is thus a node of relationships facing all directions. *Person* is a being of relationships.

The human person provides us with an analogy by which we can better understand what we mean when we speak of the divine Three as Persons. In each human existence we discover the following relationships: there is always an I-Thou relation. The I is never alone; it echoes a Thou reverberating within the I. The Thou is another I, different and open to the I of the other. It is in this play of I-Thou dialogue that the human person gradually builds his or her personality.

But the I-Thou dialogue is not all there is. There is also the communion between the I and the Thou. Communion arises when the I-and-Thou are expressed together, when they overcome the I and the Thou and together form a new relationship, the We. To say We is to reveal community. Something analogous takes place in the Blessed Trinity. The I can be signified by the Father. This I arouses a Thou, which is the Son. The Son is not simply the word *of* the Father but also the word *to* the Father. From this relationship springs the eternal dialogue. Father (I) and Son are united and reveal the We—it is the Holy Spirit. He is our Spirit, the Spirit of the Father and the Son. Hence we have here the divine union as expression of the relationship among the three divine Persons.

> "Christ reveals to us that the divine life is trinitarian communion. Father, Son, and Spirit live the supreme mystery of oneness in perfect, loving intercommunion. It is the source of all love and all other communion that gives dignity and grandeur to human existence" (Puebla document, no. 212).

27. The Trinity as an eternal self-communication

When we say that the Father, the Son, and the Holy Spirit are three divine Persons, most Christians understand the word *person* in its normal meaning: an individual who has intelligence, will, and feelings, and who can say "I." In God there would be three intelligences, three wills, three consciences. If that was all we said, and if we failed to add that the Three are always related, we would fall inevitably into the error of tritheism, meaning that we would indeed be speaking of three different gods.

Because of this difficulty presented by modern thought, two theologians, the Protestant Karl Barth and the Catholic Karl Rahner, tried to replace the word *person* in trinitarian language. Rather than helping Christians today to understand the mystery of trinitarian communion, the word *person* would seem to create more difficulties. When we simply speak of God, outside the trinitarian context, they say, we can speak of persons—otherwise we might think that God means an impersonal cosmic force. Thus God would be the absolute Person or the eternal Subject. But they have suggested that the word *person* be avoided in connection with the Blessed Trinity. In its place Barth proposed that we speak of *three modes of being*. Trinity would therefore mean that the eternal Person (God) really exists in three ways of being, as Father without origin, as Son ever generated from the Father, and as Holy Spirit, eternally coming jointly from the Father and from the Son.

Karl Rahner accepted this same intuition, giving it a little twist. Instead of speaking of *three modes of being*, he preferred to speak of *three modes of subsistence*, making this shift to avoid the error of modalism. This erroneous doctrine, as we have already pointed out, ultimately does not accept the Blessed Trinity, but rather envisions a single God revealing himself in three different manners. God would be three only for us; internally, God would be and would ever continue to be one. So Rahner says that God is a mystery of communion. God is ever coming out of God's self and surrendering in life and love. God is self-communication as radical mystery. Hence, inasmuch as self-communication in the very act of self-surrender remains sovereign and incomprehensible, a principle without principle, it is called Father; insofar as this self-communication is expressed and becomes comprehensible, and therefore is Truth, it is called Son; insofar as this self-communication welcomes in Love and creates Union, it is called the Holy Spirit. This process is not simply understood by us, but it reveals God as God is in God's self; we avoid modalism and we stand before the mystery of communion that ever takes place in three real modalities and places us within the same process, making us persons ever more capable of surrender and love.

We regard these two approaches as insufficient. First, they are very abstract. No one adores the three modes of subsistence, but rather specific persons such as the Father, the Son, and the Spirit. Second, they show God's unity but do not deal with the trinity of Persons and the relationships stirring among them. Ultimately, these approaches do not manage to escape from monotheism, and they run the risk of modalism. Our starting point is always the divine Three in communion and eternal love among themselves.

If there is a logic within the Blessed Trinity it is this: Give and give again. The three Persons are different so as to be able to give themselves to one another. And this self -giving is so perfect that the three Persons unite and are one sole God.

✑

28. The Blessed Trinity is the perfect community

At the Sixth Interecclesial Gathering of Christian Base Communities, which was held in late July 1986 in Trindade, in Central Brazil, behind the altar of the sanctuary was a huge panel on which was written: "The Blessed Trinity is the perfect community." The Blessed Trinity was represented in this manner: the Father's hands were pictured with the Holy Spirit coming from them in the form of a dove, which in turn was resting on the head of the Son, Jesus Christ. Jesus had his hands raised and was touching the hands of the Father, and he was shoulder to shoulder with representatives of the popular movements, such as the Pastoral Land Commission (CPT), the Missionary Indigenous Council (CIMI), Christian base communities, and others. The aim was to show that trinitarian communion and community is not all there is, but that along with it is human community, ever called to share in the divine communion.

This painting goes beyond a merely personal understanding of the Blessed Trinity. The divine Three—Father, Son, and Holy Spirit—obviously exist, but they do not exist only to be distinct from one another. They exist as distinct in order to be able to be joined by communion and love. What really exists is a divine community.

From all eternity, Father, Son, and Holy Spirit coexist ever together. No one comes first and no one later, no one is superior or inferior. They are equally eternal, infinite, and merciful; they make up eternal community.

When we say "community" we intend to emphasize the mutual, direct, and total relationships existing among persons; each of the persons is totally turned toward the others, and holds nothing back. Each places everything in common, including his or her being and having. Community comes from this radical communion. It is said that in the early church, as seen in the Acts of the Apostles, Christians placed everything in common; that is why there were no poor among them.

Something similar and even deeper occurs in the Blessed Trinity. The divine Three are different and irreducible; one is not the other. But none is defined while leaving out the others. Each divine Person affirms itself by affirming the other Persons, and surrendering totally to those Persons. The Persons are distinct so as to be able to surrender to the others and to be in communion. Thus there is wealth in unity and not mere uniformity. The Trinity is the model for each and every community: while individuality is respected, the community emerges through communion and mutual self-surrender. Grassroots Christians understand this well, better than any theology, and they know how to give it very accurate expression: "The Blessed Trinity is the perfect community."

In the community of the Acts of the Apostles, Christians loved one another so much that they were of one heart and one soul (Acts 4:32). If love constituted such a strong community there, how must it be with the Trinity! Speaking about this fact St. Augustine said, "Love in God is so great that it prevents inequality and creates all equality. If there can be so much love on earth and in human beings, so much so that many souls have become one alone, how is there not going to be such a love between the Father and the Son, inasmuch as both are always inseparable, and so to be one

*sole God? There many souls have become one through an
ineffable and supreme conjunction; Persons became not two
gods but a single God" (Sermon to the Catechumens on the
creed I,4; PL 40, 629).*

∽

29. Male and female within the Blessed Trinity

In Genesis, God is said to have created humankind and
to have created man and woman; he created both in his image and likeness (Gn 1:27). Only as male and female does
humankind represent God here on earth. God is beyond gender. But the human male and female find their ultimate roots
in the trinitarian mystery. Because the Trinity-God is male
and female, we as men and women can be its image and likeness.

In recent years many Christians, especially women, have
realized that theological language presents almost everything
in male terms. God is Father, who eternally generates a Son,
and together they are the ever-giving origin to the Holy
Spirit. The main ideas in Christianity are male, and only
men—women are excluded—have leadership in the church
and are ordained in the sacrament of orders.

Based on the truth of the faith that each human person
(male and female) is image and likeness of God, many have
wondered: Could we not overcome sexist language (using
only terms representative of one sex, that is, the male) and
come to use a discourse that would be beyond gender and
utilize the values of both genders to express the wealth of
the mystery of God? Indeed, more and more Christians are
trying to avoid speaking only of "man" when they mean humankind and are learning to say "man and woman" or simply

"human" or "human person." Likewise, they avoid speaking of God just as Father; they are also introducing the word *Mother*. Indeed, Pope John Paul I in a public audience said, "God is Father, but is primarily Mother." The Old Testament prophets used expressions that symbolized God as Mother who lifts people up to her breast, kisses them, and wipes away their tears (Hos 11:4; Is 49:15, 66:13; Ps 25:6). To the Hebrew mind, saying that God is merciful means saying that God is like a mother who has a heart and takes pity on her sons and daughters, just as every mother has mercy on her sons and her daughters. In his encyclical *Rich in Mercy* Pope John Paul II reminds us of this feminine dimension of the Father. So we can say that God the Father has motherly traits, and God the Mother has fatherly traits. God is simultaneously Father and infinitely tender Mother. We could say something similar of the Son and the Holy Spirit. They are co-source of the female and the male. In their activity in salvation history, they show these male and female traits in the lives of just men and women. They are accordingly close to each of us and enwrap us in their own reality. Our male and female identities are inserted into the eternal Male and Female in resplendent communion.

> *What is our future as men and women? It is not enough to say that we will arise to eternal life; that does not slake our infinite thirst. Each woman and each man who arrives at the reign of the Trinity will participate as man and as woman in the trinitarian Community itself. The female and the male that make us image and likeness of the Trinity (Gn 1:27) will be united in the Eternal Female and Eternal Male.*

30. Father, Son, and Holy Spirit exist together from all eternity

The Father, the Son, and the Holy Spirit, are three Unique Ones, united in life, love, and eternal communion. Hence they are not three gods but one sole God. They emerge simultaneously, they eternally break forth toward one another, constituting a single community of life, love, and union. It is like three streams whose waters run out to meet one another, constituting a single lake. It is as though three waterspouts were to shoot upward and meet on top forming a single torrential jet of water—and to do so eternally. The fathers in the church councils rightfully insist on reaffirming that each divine Person is equally eternal, equally powerful, equally immense. Everything in the Trinity is simultaneous. No one is greater or higher, lower or lesser, prior or subsequent. The divine Three are coequal from all eternity. By reason of this root equality, the divine Persons are concomitant. How are they unified and one sole God?

What constitutes the union among the divine Persons is the uninterrupted and infinite interpenetration of Father, Son, and Holy Spirit. This is something we have already considered, perichoresis, one Person being in the others, and each Person permeating and being permeated by the other two. This union is specific to persons and spiritual beings. Only persons who are different from one another can establish relationships of intimacy, mutual surrender, and love that ground a communion and a community. The communion among the divine Persons is absolute, and the relationship is infinite. This living together and existing together constitute the unity of what is called the divine essence or nature or substance. If we look closely, it is constituted by love. St.

John affirmed: "God is love" (1 Jn 4:8, 16). St. Augustine said that the eternal love among the divine Three grounds trinitarian union. With expressions whose secret only he knew, he wrote: "Each of the divine Persons is in each of the others, and all are in each, and each is in all, and all are in all, and all are only one God." Therefore, if the church's doctrine says that the equal nature in each of the divine Persons constitutes unity in God, then we must understand this nature, in keeping with New Testament revelation, as love and infinite intercommunion. The Trinity of Persons is a fundamental fact about the divine existence. It is not the product of the absolute Spirit developing outward or the internal differentiation of an ever-equal divine nature. God is eternally, without beginning or end, Father, Son and Holy Spirit, reciprocity of the divine Three in a single love, infinite in-breaking of a single life.

> *"In the Blessed Trinity what is it but love that preserves that supreme and ineffable unity? Love is the law and this law is the law of the Lord. This love constitutes the Trinity in unity and in some fashion unifies the Persons in the bond of Peace. Love creates love. This is the love that governs the universe, a law that creates all and governs all"* (St. Bernard, Book of the Love of God, *chap. 12, no. 35; PL 182, 996 B).*

✍

31. In the Trinity all relationships are threefold

Father, Son, and Holy Spirit are co-eternal and simultaneous. How to make it clear that each of the Persons is different from the others and yet interrelated? Taking off from the New Testament, theology speaks of divine processions.

It thereby wishes to show how one Person is related to the other. The Father is said to be source and cause of the entire godhead. From him proceed the Son and the Holy Spirit. The Father is also said to *generate* the Son. Father and Son *spirate* the Holy Spirit as from a single principle. These expressions—*cause, generation, spiration,* and *processions*—may give us the impression that in God there is some sort of *theogony* (genesis and generation of God). Can we really say that the principle of causality is valid in the Trinity? That there is a generation and a spiration? Do we not always say that the divine Persons are originally simultaneous, and that they eternally coexist in communion and interpenetration (perichoresis)? From the standpoint of eternity, the Father is not prior to the Son and to the Holy Spirit. They always break forth together and already interrelated in love and infinite communion.

By reason of this concomitance of the divine Persons, we must understand the expressions used by the church and taken up by theology—such as *cause, generation,* and *spiration*—in an analogous and figurative sense. We are dealing with formulas that are highly suggestive. They show how the divine Three are always *respective,* that is, one is in respect to the other. Indeed, the Father does not exist without the Son, or the Son without the Father. The Breath (Spirit) does not exist except as accompanying the Word (Son) spoken by the mouth of the Father. If we use canonized expressions, it is always in a strictly trinitarian sense; it is valid only for the trinitarian mystery, where everything is eternal, concomitant, and simultaneous. But we grant that there is a risk that they will be understood anthropomorphically (as though it were something human, such as generation, etc.) and inadequately for the mystery of the divine Three.

There is another possibility, likewise flowing from the scripture: speaking of the divine Persons in terms of revelation and recognition. The co-eternal and coequal Persons are revealed reciprocally, and they recognize one another and are recognized in each other and by one another. Thus the Father is revealed through the Son in the Spirit. The Son reveals the Father in the power of the Spirit. The Holy Spirit proceeds from the Father and reposes on the Son. Thus, the Spirit is of the Father through the Son (*a Patre Filioque*) as the Son is recognized in the Father through the love of the Spirit (*a Patre Spirituque*). By reason of this enfolding of the three Persons in one another, we must say that the relationships among them are always threefold: wherever one Person is, the other two are always there as well.

> *How much concord, how much joy, and how much justice would there be in this world if we were to embrace trinitarian logic in our thinking and acting: ever inclusive, ever involving, ever communitarian, ever accepting of difference and keeping it from becoming inequality?*

∽

32. Three suns but a single light: Such is the Blessed Trinity

Many Christians find it particularly difficult to imagine the three divine Persons being a single God. How can three equal one? We must say, as we did at the outset, that when we speak of three Persons and only one God we are not engaged in any sort of mathematics or accounting operation. The scriptures never count anything in God. They are only familiar with the expression *unique*. The Father is unique, the Son is unique, and the Holy Spirit is unique. *Unique* is not a number, the first of a series, but precisely the denial of any number. Nothing is like or subsequent to what is unique—it is alone and there is no other. Hence there is no addition at work in the Blessed Trinity.

This must be our starting point: There are three Unique Ones, the Father, the Son, and the Holy Spirit. This is an important statement. The basis of all reality rests on the co-existence of three Unique Ones and not on the solitude of the One, ever identical to Itself. The three Unique Ones cannot be reduced to each other. They are distinct but not unequal. Similarly, there is samba, rock, bossa nova, and Gregorian chant, which are different genres of music, but they are not unequal in dignity and value. Difference is not synonymous with inequality. All are expressions of music. Something similar happens with the three Unique Ones. They are distinct—the Father is not the Son or the Holy Spirit—but they are equally eternal and equally God. If they are distinct, it is so that they can be in communion and share their own wealth with one another. The three Unique Ones are never juxtaposed, one up against the others. The divine Three are eternally toward one another. Indeed, they live within one another, they share life and love with one another in such an infinite and perfect way that they constitute a single community. That is why we say, without violating logic and mathematics, that the three divine Persons are related in such a way that they lovingly permeate one another so radically and so completely, that they constitute a single God.

If we are to be able to understand this unity, we must consider the human experiences of love and intimacy in connection with the spirit, the heart, and persons. Two people love each other, and in the family there are three (father, mother, and child). But their attraction is so deep that they feel they form a single life and a single merging of hearts and destiny. Something similar and infinitely more perfect takes place with the divine Three: the love, the communion among them, and the circulation of life of each one, ever and eternally surrendered to the others, are so absolute that they constitute the unity of God. As St. John Damascene said: The Blessed Trinity is like three suns. They are within one another in such a way that they give out a single light. Thus, God is both three Persons and eternally a single loving God.

> To glimpse a little of the mystery of communion of the divine Three, we must descend deeply into our own experiences. We must heed the call of love that desires union, communion, and to merge with the person loved. Deep down, we do not want to keep saying, "I think, I want, I do," but "we think, we want, we do," together and in communion. If that is the way it is with us, pale image of the Trinity, it will be so much more true among the Father, the Son, and the Holy Spirit, three Persons and a single God-of-love-and-life, true prototype of everything that is and lives.

cᴑ

✍ VI ✍

The communion of the Trinity: Critique and inspiration for society and church

33. *Beyond capitalism and real socialism*

The communion among Father, Son, and Holy Spirit, constituting one God, is a mystery of inclusion. The three divine Persons open to outside and invite human beings and the entire universe to share in their community and their life. Jesus said it marvelously—" . . . so that all may be one. As you, Father, are in me and I am in you, may they also be in us" (Jn 17:21). The presence of trinitarian communion in history makes it possible for the barriers that turn difference into inequality and discrimination to be overcome; thus, in the mystery of the Son (second Person of the Trinity), there is neither Jew nor pagan, men nor women—all are one (Gal 3:28). Economically, all goods are shared (Acts 4:31-35), and socially, all are "of one heart and one soul" (Acts 4:32). Such things are of a utopian nature: they are ideals toward which we are headed. They unleash energies so that we may reach ever greater levels of participation and communion, and at the same time we relativize and critique every conquest attained, keeping it open for further improvements.

There is a fundamental human yearning for sharing, equality, respect for differences, and communion of all and with God. The communion of the divine Three offers a source of inspiration for achieving these age-old yearnings of all people and all societies. Each divine Person shares fully in the other two: in life, love, and communion. Each is equal in eternity, majesty, and dignity; none is superior or inferior to the others. Although equal in sharing in life and love, each Person is distinct from the others. The Father is distinct from the Son and from the Holy Spirit, and so it is with each Person. But this distinction allows for communion and mutual self-giving. The Persons are distinct so as to be able to give out of their wealth to the others and to form eternal communion and divine community. The Blessed Trinity is the most wonderful community.

How to realize this ideal in our dominant social systems today, capitalism and socialism? Capitalism is grounded in the individual and his or her personal performance, with no essential tie to others and society. In capitalism goods are appropriated privately, leaving out the vast majority. Difference is valued at the expense of communion. In socialism it is the sharing of all that is valued—and hence it is structurally closer to God's design than any other system—but personal differences are little valued. Society tends to mean *mass* rather than a network of communities in which persons count. The trinitarian mystery beckons us toward social forms in which all relations between persons and institutions are valued, in an egalitarian way, one of kinship and respect for differences. Only thus will oppression be overcome and life and freedom triumph.

Present and working in all radically human and social prob-
lems lies an infinite dream, an ultimate demand of life for
all, justice for all, starting with the least, and a demand for
the inclusion of all and for communion with everything and
with all. In other words, there is always a theological ques-
tion that has to do with the Supreme, the Decisive, in our
history. This is the emergence of the mystery of the Trinity
in which the three Persons, out of mutual love, converge to
the point of being a single, living, life-giving God.

☙

34. From a church-as-society to a church-as-communion

The church has a dimension of mystery that can be grasped
only through faith. It is bearer of the memory of Jesus Christ,
the power of the Spirit, and the tradition of the apostles. We
believe that in it the substance of the incarnation is contin-
ued in history; through Christ and the Holy Spirit, God is
definitively close to each of us and within human history.
This mystery becomes embodied in history, because it is organized in groups and communities. Communities in turn
assume the elements of each age, so that the church has as
many faces as the incarnations it has undergone throughout
history. The monarchical conception of power has been the
one that has most deeply marked the church and how it arranges the distribution of power among it members. Pre-
trinitarian or non-trinitarian monotheism has weighed more
heavily here than trinitarian thinking. Even today it is said
that just as there is one God, just as there is one Christ, so
there ought to exist on earth one sole official representative
of Christ—the pope for the whole church, the bishop for

the diocese, the pastor for the parish, and the coordinator for the base community. A great deal of power is thereby being concentrated in a single figure. In relating to others such persons inevitably assume a paternalistic attitude and a handout mindset. Those wielding power feel invested with huge responsibilities, for they must represent God before others, wielding this power for the sake of others and for their eternal salvation. They will do everything *for* the people. And as only they are God's official representatives, they are unlikely to act *with* the people or *out of* the people. Thus, they cease to recognize and value the intelligence of the people, their experience of faith, their ability to evangelize, and their character as also representing God and Christ. This monarchical practice is likely to give rise to authoritarianism matched by subservience. There is a shift from a church-as-communion-of-believers, all equal and sharing responsibility, to a church-as-society, with unequal distribution of functions and tasks.

If, however, we take as our starting point that the Blessed Trinity is the perfect community, and that the communion of the divine Three makes them one God, then we will see another type of church emerge. It is fundamentally community. Each one has his or her own characteristics and gifts, but all live for the good of all. There arises a community with diversities that are respected and valued as expression of the wealth of community of the Trinity itself. Each one, insofar as he or she creates community and becomes part of that communion, represents the Blessed Trinity. In the Trinity what unites the divine Three is the communion among them and the complete self-giving of one Person to the others. The same thing ought to happen in the church. It is by overcoming the centralization of power and distributing it among all that dynamic unity emerges, reflecting trinitarian union.

When the church forgets the source that gives it birth—the communion of the three divine Persons—it allows its unity to become uniformity; it lets one group of believers by itself assume all responsibilities, keeping others from participating; it allows its confessional interests to prevail over the interests of the reign; in short, the river of bright waters is in danger of becoming a stagnant pond. We must be converted to the Trinity to recover diversity and communion, which create the dynamic unity that is ever open to new enrichment.

⌘

✑ VII ✑

The Person of the Father: Mystery of tenderness

35. Who is the Father? Mystery of tenderness

Jesus said, "No one knows the Father except the Son and anyone to whom the Son chooses to reveal him" (Mt 11:27). The Father is an unfathomable mystery. The Father is invisible. He becomes visible through his Son (Jn 1:18, 14:9). We are therefore dependent on Jesus, the only-begotten Son, in order to get some glimpse of the Father's face. To begin with, Jesus makes it clear that the Father is a mystery of tenderness. He calls him *Abba*. Jesus is so close to the Father that he says, "All mine are yours" (Jn 17:10), and "The Father and I are one" (Jn 10:30). Hence, "Whoever has seen me has seen the Father" (Jn 14:9).

Moreover, the Son shows how the Father acts by building the reign, giving life, being merciful, and showing his Providence. The Father's great cause is the establishment of the reign. This means: death shall reign no more, division shall not prevail, justice and universal kinship will win out. With his own practice Jesus seeks to strengthen the implementation of this cause of the Father: "The Son can do . . . only what he sees the Father doing" (Jn 5:19). In the reign, life triumphs for good. This is a God of life who always takes the side of those who need life. Both the Father and Jesus strive to generate life, and life in abundance (Jn 10:10). Hence Jesus says, "Just as the Father raises the dead and gives them life, so also the Son gives life to whomever he wishes" (Jn 5:21). The Father shows mercy to those who have lost life through sin, as is well expressed in the parable of the prodigal son (Lk 15:11-32). He continues always to love the ungrateful and evil (Lk 5:32), because his nature is love, and when he does not see his love returned, he offers mercy. Moreover, he is a Father full of Providence. He cares for the hairs of every human head, causes the lilies to grow in all their splendor, and watches over the little birds in the air (Lk 21:18; Mt 6:26-30).

Finally, the Father shows how he is in relation to his Son Jesus. He loved us so much that he delivered up his own Son. The Son has shown himself to be one who most presses forward the reign; he devoted himself to the life of those who were weakest, healing, consoling, and raising the dead; he showed mercy toward the woman who was a public sinner and toward all those who sought forgiveness for their sins. The tenderness of Jesus toward all who sought him out reflected the tenderness of the Father. Hence, he could say, "Everything that the Father gives me will come to me, and anyone who comes to me I will never drive away" (Jn 6:37). He did not send away the children, or Nicodemus who sought him out at night, or the Pharisees who invited him to eat, or the Samaritan woman, or those who cried out to him for help from afar. He accepted all, imitating the heavenly Father, who takes in all as his sons and daughters.

The most frightful and unbearable feeling is rejection, knowing that we are not accepted. It is like being a "stranger in

the nest," experiencing psychological death. When I say
"Father," I seek to express the conviction that there is someone who accepts me absolutely. My moral situation matters
little, I can always trust that there awaits a parental lap to
receive me. There I will not be a stranger but a child, even
if prodigal, in my Father's house.

∽

36. The Father, eternal root
of all sister-and-brotherhood

The Father is the one who is eternally, even before any
creature existed. If, hypothetically, we could imagine that
there had been no creation, and no created being existed,
the Father would still be Father. It is not because he is Creator that the Father is Father. There might be a Creator who
would have been a single God, a single infinite Person, without being Father. The Father is Father because he is Father
of the only-begotten Son, because from all eternity he is in
communion with the Son in the Holy Spirit, because he is
"generating" the eternal Son in the power of the Spirit. From
a trinitarian standpoint, fatherhood is proper to the Father.
In generating the Son, the Father projects out from himself
all things that can imitate him and the Son. In the Son thus
generated are sketched all other sons and daughters created
in the image and likeness of the Father, Son, and Holy Spirit.
Hence there is an eternal and filial dimension in creation.
With the love that generates the Son, the Father gives origin to all other beings in the Son, through the Son, with the
Son, and for the Son (Jn 1:3; Col 1:15-17). All beings share
in the filiation of the only-begotten Son and in the spiration
of the Holy Spirit.

Because we all exist in the Son (cf. Rom 8:29), we are all brothers and sisters. Christ, eternal Son, is the "firstborn within a large family" (Rom 8:29). Hence, God is Father and we are brothers and sisters, not primarily because God is Creator and has created us, but because he is Father of the only-begotten Son (Rom 15:6; 1 Cor 1:3; 2 Cor 11:31; Eph 3:14). And we were envisioned in the eternal Son by the Father in the same movement of love with which the Father "generated" the Son in union with the Holy Spirit. Thus we are not mere creatures foreign to the trinitarian mystery. Our kinship is rooted in the very mystery of the Father's fecundity. To mark the difference between the eternal Son and his brothers and sisters, theology uses the expressions *only-begotten* Son and *adoptive* sons and daughters. The Son is not created but generated out of the very substance of love and communion of the Father together with the Spirit. We, brothers and sisters of the only-begotten Son, are created out of nothing in the image and likeness of the Son by the Father, together with the Spirit. In any case, the Son's Father is our Father. Jesus has correctly taught us to call him "our Father who art in heaven." The Father is never without the Son. And the Son is never without the Father's other adoptive sons and daughters, and hence he is never without his brothers and sisters. This vision runs counter to all authoritarianism and paternalism based solely on the figure of the creator God, Father of the universe. This God first generated the Son and all of us in him. It accordingly follows that the community of equals, brothers and sisters, is the true representative of the Trinity. Hence, if there is authority, it is to enhance community, in service within it, and ever with it.

It is fascinating to know that we existed before existing; that we were in the mind of the Father; that we have been loved eternally; that also over each one of us the Father has said what he said, says, and will forever say to his only-begotten Son: "You are my beloved son and daughter. In you I have placed all my affection."

↶↷

37. Motherly Father, and fatherly Mother

When Christian faith proclaims that God is Father of the eternal Son together with the Holy Spirit, it intends to express that in him we experience the absolute mystery from which everything comes and toward which everything is going. He is the source of all fruitfulness. This idea can be expressed by the terms *Father* and *Mother*. The words are different, but the concept (what is thought) is the same. By saying eternal Father and Mother we also intend to say that the female and the male, which are the image and likeness of God according to Genesis (1:27), find in the Blessed Trinity their ultimate root and justification. Some Christians may not be used to such terminology, for we are heirs to the predominance of the male and of sexist language about God. But if we look at the Bible, we will note that God is presented along lines proper to a mother. The Council of Toledo (675) teaches that "we must believe that the Son does not proceed from nothing nor from some other substance, but has been generated and born *from the womb of the Father,* that is, from his substance." The text speaks about a womb, but it is women who have wombs. God is a motherly Father and a fatherly Mother. In other words, God's fecundity is better expressed by these two human sources of fruitfulness, namely, the earthly father and earthly mother. Both worthily express what God is in God's own mystery, which originates everything, God, who underlies the whole process of generation and the emergence of new being.

The prophet Isaiah presented God as a mother, saying,

> Can a woman forget her nursing child,
>   or show no compassion for the child of
>   her womb? (Is 49:15).

This is all the more so with God. A mother's basic stance is to console and wipe away the tears from her sons and daughters. Thus, the same prophet says,

> As a mother comforts her child,
>   so I will comfort you (Is 66:13).

One of God's basic characteristics is to be merciful. In the Hebrew mind, *merciful* means "being like a mother inside." The father of the prodigal son reveals motherly traces: he runs out to meet his son, embraces him, and covers him with kisses. Thus we can say that God is only eternal Father if he also displays motherly features. He is only Mother of eternal tenderness if he also reveals fatherly aspects. In the Father and Mother we feel fully sheltered in the trusting reign of sons and daughters, free and happy, members of the divine family.

> *It is most comforting to discover that the Father is only fully Father when he is also shown as Mother. Like the father of the prodigal son, God is waiting for us, looking toward the bend in the road, in order to run out to meet us, to embrace us and cover us with kisses. But for all that to happen, we have to yearn for our fatherly and motherly house and decide to return.*

⌒♡⌒

38. The Father, principle without principle

The incarnate Son's revelation of the eternal Father to us enables us to glimpse something of his immanent reality. We only know the Father through the Son's revelation (Mt 11:27), insofar as the Father represents the depth of mystery par excellence. Each of the Persons is mystery, but in the Father the mystery emerges as mystery. Obviously, the divine mystery is always a mystery of communion, life, and love. Rather than terrifying us, it is something that fascinates us and invites us to share in its happiness. Faith says that the Father is the principle without principle. Like the other Persons, he is a source pouring forth life from all eternity. He communicates this life in fullness. That is why we believe that the Father "generates" the Son in the Holy Spirit. As we already reflected, the term *to generate* does not mean a duplication of the Father; it is how the Father reveals himself in the eternal Son and shows his fruitfulness in him. The Father is also together with the Holy Spirit, "spirating" the Spirit in union with the only-begotten Son. This spiration does not mean that the Father, in conjunction with the Son, causes the third Person, the Holy Spirit. The Holy Spirit unites Father and Son in the love that permeates the three divine Persons. Because the divine Three are always together, we pray equally to the Three the same prayer: "Glory be to the Father, glory be to the Son, glory be to the Holy Spirit."

The entire mystery of the Trinity defies human reason, not only now while we are here on earth, but even in eternity and forever. Yet this mystery is ever open to understanding and sharing. Hence the mystery is Father insofar as it is without root and is root of all else; it is also Son, insofar as it is revealed and is displayed to the outside as truth; and it is also Holy Spirit insofar as it unifies all and surrenders itself as love. When we speak of the Father, we are referring to the ultimate horizon of all, the One who contains all and illumines all. From him it is possible to receive the Person of the Son and of the Holy Spirit. They are always together and are simultaneous. But so that we may understand something of the Blessed Trinity in the form of fragile signs and slight hints, we must always begin with the Father. He is the first of the simultaneous ones when we want to establish a certain order among the trinitarian Persons—first the Father, second the Son, and third the Holy Spirit. This language is ours as expression of faith. But we must know that actually none is prior or is superior, but that the Three are coequal, co-eternal, and co-loving. Yet it is in the mystery of the Father that this mystery, which is equal in each Person, is singularly made manifest.

> The eye can see all but cannot see itself. Every river goes back to its source but the source does not go back to anything; it springs forth by itself. The mystery of the Father is like that. He is the hidden source that makes everything possible and from which everything begins. He is always present, although invisible, present to produce life and defend anything whose life is in jeopardy.

∽

39. How the Father appears: In the mystery of all things

The Blessed Trinity is fully present in creation. Each divine Person appears in its distinction and specific property. How does the Father appear as Father in our world? We have already noted that in the Father we glimpse the boundless mystery of the entire Blessed Trinity. The Father represents the first and the last, origin and end. The Father signifies fruitfulness, the generation and ultimate source of anything that can exist. He is fundamentally the beginning without beginning, together with those who are simultaneous: Son and Holy Spirit. To say that the Father is origin and principle of all means something incomprehensible to us. Our knowledge is always of that which has already begun and has already been originated. Hence, we always come later; we can never be present at our own origin. We owe our life to a mystery. Hence, whatever has to do with origin, such as the issuing forth of new life and the emergence of anything new, has to do with the Father, source and origin of all. Everything that challenges us and presents itself as a mystery sends us a sign of the Father in creation.

The existence of the universe is a mystery; it need not exist and yet it exists. Human life in personal form, the individual path of each life, what happens in the depths of the human heart, and the ultimate meaning of everything that exists are mystery. All these pointers that are enshrouded in mystery point back to the mystery of the Father. The Father is present in such experiences. He is present in our own mystery, because we are ever in search of a final port of call or ultimate welcome. The questioning never ceases: Where did we come from? What are we doing here on earth? Where are we going? We intuit more than we know, for we remain in indecipherable mystery. It is the Father who dwells in us when we stir up such hints.

Sometimes we are plunged into radical crisis; we feel lost. Sometimes an entire people is laid low because it has been defeated and it has seen its identity destroyed. It has to start over and begin its journey anew. In such a situation of crisis Jesus cried out to God, calling him, "my Father" (Mt 26:39,

42); the people of Israel after being freed from slavery in Egypt discovered God as Father (Is 63:16). They experienced the God who hears the cry of his oppressed children. God was revealed as *o goel*, which means "Father-God," avenger of the unjustly oppressed.

It is particularly the poor and humiliated who sense God as Father (and godfather[1]), for no one is on their side but God. Jesus himself, Son of the Father, made these least ones the primary addressees of his liberating message. In his closeness to the Father he discovered the liberating dimension of the mystery of the Father. He did what the Father has always done, is doing, and will do in history: he takes the side of those who are unjustly defeated in order to bring them under his protection. Hence the Father becomes present in those whose character as children is most denied. He appears in all those who set out to struggle for a more family-like world (where all are children and all brothers and sisters).

Is not everything charged with mystery? The starry sky, the streetlight, a child's smile, the gesture to aid a person with a disability, the hand opened up to give. It is the mystery of the Father who comes forth and leaves us signs.

❧

---

[1] Boff's addition of *godfather*, which perhaps seems strange in English, is suggestive in a Latin American context where the godparent relationship is taken seriously. Poor parents may seek someone powerful, a landholder or government figure, whose wealth or access to power may someday offer protection in a social context where one's own father may be weak.—TRANS.

VIII

The Person of the Son:
Mystery of communication
and principle of liberation

40. Who is the Son? Eternal communication

Alongside—and eternally communicating with—the Father is the Son. He is the full expression of the Father. The Father recognizes himself in the Son, in his eternity and in his mystery of tenderness. The Son shows distinction and yet communion in God. Hence Father and Son are ever together, knowing one another, recognizing and surrendering to one another. The Son became incarnate to bring creation to fullness by way of redemption. Through his incarnation he has revealed to us the mystery of communion that is the triune God. As already noted, in the midst of persons, acting in a liberating manner, the Son has revealed the Father to us; the transforming drive that he radiated indicated the presence of the Holy Spirit. How did Jesus of Nazareth, that poor man in solidarity with all who suffer, reveal to us the second Person of the Blessed Trinity, the Son? If we take the gospels as they are written, it is not hard to see: The Son is there with all his intense presence as revealer of the Father's secrets, as mediator of full liberation for all, beginning with the poor, in the power of the Spirit who dwells in him. However, our New Testament texts gather not only the words and deeds of Jesus, but also the reflections of the early Christian communities on the Jesus event. Today, it is not easy to distinguish what comes from the Jesus of history and what comes from his followers. The important thing is that both Jesus and the thoughts of the early Christians clearly witness that we stand before the Son of God. This Son of God set up his tent in the midst of our misery.

First, Jesus shows himself Son of God in prayer. He always invokes God as *Abba*. The one calling God Father feels he is Son. He has taught us to likewise call him Father and to understand ourselves as sons and daughters, and hence as brothers and sisters. Second, Jesus acts as the Father's Son. He accepts being a representation of the Father; as the Father works to the present, he also works (Jn 5:17). Just as the Father is merciful, he also is merciful. He forgives sins, and by living with sinners he grants them the certainty of the Father's forgiveness. Third, he obeys the Father's plan, which is to set up the reign, to the point of death, even when he is tempted; he faithfully holds out in the face of all persecution; even when raised on the cross in utter abandonment, he confidently surrenders to the Father.

In the enthusiasm that he arouses in the people, in the courage to overcome obsolete traditions, in the life he stirs up wherever he goes, he enables us to see that the Spirit dwells in him and also reveals him to the world. Jesus is thus the Son of the Father in the Spirit and also our marvelous elder Brother.

The logic of hands is more convincing than the logic of words. To be revealed as Son of the eternal Father, Jesus has privileged deeds over speech. He performed liberating deeds, pardoned sins, and raised the dead. Rather than saying, "I am the Son of God," Jesus acted as the Son of God.

༄

41. The eternal Son of the eternal Father in the Holy Spirit

Who is the eternal Son in himself? Faith tells us he is the unbegotten Son of the Father, of the same substance as the Father. He is not created but "generated without beginning and without principle," and "subsists in the Father from all eternity." How the Father "generates" the Son without being prior to him remains shrouded in mystery for us, for Father and Son are coequal and equally eternal. What we can say with certainty is that Father and Son live in the same communion-nature. They are distinct in order to be able to surrender to each other mutually and to live out an eternal union. St. John says that the Son is the Word. He expresses the entire reality of the Father. Paul says that Jesus is "the image of the invisible God" (Father) (Col 1:15). The entire divine mysteriousness is communicated and projected in the Son. He is the Intelligence of the mystery shared by the three divine Persons. Hence, the Son is preeminently the divine revelation and communication within the Trinity and in creation. The Father gives all he has to the Son—except for the Father's being Father. The Son will also receive from the Father the capacity to spirate the Holy Spirit. Father and Son together make possible the emergence of the Holy Spirit. When we use these expressions—*generation, spiration, give rise, allow the emergence*—we must immediately confess our inadequacy; the words are not adequate because they give the impression of succession and causality, when actually everything takes place in the dimension of eternity, where there is neither beginning nor end. Hence, we must stress the simultaneity of the divine Three; they coexist and are in communion with each other eternally. Ever subsisting in them is perichoresis, that is, the interpenetration of life, giving, and love. Hence, the Son, in being "generated" by the Father, simultaneously receives the Holy Spirit, who rests upon him and is ever joined with him. Son and Holy Spirit therefore come to creation together, so as to bring it to fullness and fully liberate it. Together with the Holy Spirit, the Father relates and reveals himself to the Son. The Son and the Holy Spirit together discover the innascibility of the Father and reveal it to us.

The Son is incarnate in our history. He thereby confers a character of son and daughter on all creatures, primarily human beings. In some sense now that the risen Son is back in the Trinity, something of our nature is made eternal and definitively enters into eternal life, love, and communion. If he is Son of the Father, united to the Spirit, we are sons and daughters in the Son and all brothers and sisters in the power of that same Spirit.

As dire as the human journey may appear, something of it is absolutely preserved and radically fulfilled: the sacred humanity of Jesus, assumed by the eternal Son, is definitively brought into the bosom of the Trinity. Something of ours, of our heart, of our infinite desire, is forever saved through Jesus.

ॐ

42. The male and female of the Son and our Brother

Genesis reveals to us that we are images and likenesses of God as men and women (Gn 1:27). This entails recognizing that the ultimate roots of our personal reality, whether male or female, are found in the very mystery of God. The divine Persons do not have sex; they are beyond such created characteristics. But the values and dimensions communicated by the male and the female are also divine values. Hence, we can consider the female and male dimensions of each of the divine Persons. In Jesus we find the perfect integration of the female and the male. First, of the male, because Jesus was not a woman, but a man. However, like any man, he included in himself the female dimension, which he certainly expressed. The whole thrust of Jesus, his ability to opt for the poor, those to whom he primarily addressed his message, his courage in facing opposition, and his very death, reveal his male side, which is also present in women, but differently. The female expresses the tender side of male and female human life: care, mercy, sensitivity to the mystery of life, particularly toward those who have less, and the innerness of prayer. The gospel accounts present Jesus as someone who had integrated the *anima* (female dimension) within his *animus* (male dimension). He maintains a deeply human and tender relationship toward the women who cross his path, several of whom are disciples (Lk 10:38-42). He is forever stepping in to defend a woman in need, like the adulteress, the Syro-Phoenician woman who begs for help, the Samaritan woman, the woman bent over, and the woman who was hemorrhaging.

With very feminine attitudes he takes pity on the poor whom he meets on the highway; he is filled with compassion (he is stirred internally) over the people who are abandoned (Mk 6:34), he does not hold back from tears when he learns that his friend Lazarus is dead (Jn 11:35). In a very female way he says that he wanted to gather the children of Jerusalem like a hen gathers her chicks under her wings and they were unwilling (Lk 13:34).

This female dimension of Jesus is part of his humanity. This humanity was hypostatically assumed by the eternal Son. This means that something of the female is divinized forever. Women are also called to share in the life of eternal communion and to find in each person of the Blessed Trinity a prototype for their efforts at growth and betterment.

Inside every human being is something of the female and male dimensions, both tenderness and strength. One of life's challenges is to integrate both dimensions so that we are fully human, and hence reflections of God. Jesus took on and integrated his male and female sides. The eternal Son incarnate in him sanctified and divinized these two dimensions forever.

ब्ळ

43. The mission of the Son: Liberate and make all sons and daughters

The Son has been sent to the world by the Father together with the Holy Spirit. He not only enlightens everyone who comes into this world (Jn 1:9), but he has visited us in our own flesh, becoming our brother in our situation of poverty and oppression. What is the ultimate meaning of the coming and the mission of the Son among us? What is the intention of the Eternal One? Two currents have contended for the best interpretation. One of them takes as its starting point the part of the creed that says, "For our salvation (the Son) came down from heaven and was conceived by the Holy Spirit." In this vision the incarnation was prompted by the sin of humankind, which separated us from God. Sin occupies the center. In order to redeem us from this sin, the Father has sent us his own Son. We ask, Is it worthy of God to allow sin to occupy so central a place? Is not God and his glory the center of all? Hence, the other approach takes as its starting point an understanding based on the prologue to John's gospel, the epistles to the Ephesians and Colossians, and some statements in the epistle to the Hebrews. It is said that "all things came into being through him, and without him not one thing came into being" (Jn 1:3). St. Paul says that God's plan is to "gather up all things in him" (Eph 1:10). Hence it could be said that "all things have been created through him and for him; He himself is before all things, and in him all things hold together" (Col 1:16; cf. Heb 2:7-8). In other words, the incarnation is not an emergency solution to redirect creation back to the original path from which it had strayed. The incarnation of the Son belongs to the mystery of creation. Without the coming of the Son, everything would be without a head, and therefore without an ultimate meaning and without an ultimate crowning.

We believe that this second approach better interprets the divine mysteries in keeping with the divine glorification itself. The Son "verbifies"; that is, he makes the entire universe share in his nature as Word, makes sons and daughters of all beings in creation, including nonhumans. Because of the sin of human beings, which has also contaminated relationships with nature, the incarnation took place in the form of humiliation and not of glory, but this modality does not change the essence of the plan of the Blessed Trinity: to bring the entire universe into communion.

This vision squares better with a truly divine understanding of creation. As already noted, in projecting himself in the Son and being revealed in him, the Father projects and reveals all possible resemblances of himself and his Son that might some day be created. In this sense creation is already within the Blessed Trinity as plan. The sacred humanity of Jesus is there, capable of gathering into the full communion of the Son when he would be sent to enter into our history. And he came. That event signals the beginning of our blessed end: we are now within the Blessed Trinity!

Everything bears the marks of the Son, because everything has been made in him, with him, and for him. The scrap in the street, the star in the sky, and the atomic particle are like children, because they are in the Son. They are also our brothers and sisters. Hence, we respect and love them as we do ourselves.

cそ๑

IX

The Person of the Holy Spirit: Mystery of love, and in-breaking of the new

44. Who is the Holy Spirit?
The driving force of full liberation

The Holy Spirit is the one who surpasses the I-Thou relationship (Father-Son) and brings in the We. That is why the Holy Spirit is the union par excellence among the divine Persons, the Person who reveals most clearly to us the eternal and essential interrelating among the divine Three. The Spirit in history appears as a volcanic force, as a windstorm that seizes people and leads them to do great works. That happens with charismatic leaders like the Judges, the prophets, and the Suffering Servant, who struggle to reestablish right and justice; the kings, who are invested with power to protect the people; and the Messiah, bearer of all the gifts of the Spirit. Some features of the Spirit should be highlighted.

The Spirit is the power of the new and of the renewal of all things, creating order in creation, causing the new Adam to spring from Mary's womb, impelling Jesus to evangelize, raising the Crucified One from the dead, anticipating the new humankind in the church, and in the end, bringing us the new heaven and new earth.

It is the Spirit who updates the memory of Jesus the Liberator. He never allows Jesus' words to remain dead; whenever they are reread, they gain new meaning and produce new practices.

The Spirit is the liberating principle freeing us from the oppressions of our sinful situation, which the Bible calls flesh. *Flesh* expresses the life-project of persons turned in on themselves, forgetful of others and of God. Spirit always produces freedom (cf. 2 Cor 3:17), self-surrender to others, and love. The Spirit is the father of the poor, imbuing them with hope that they can shake off the oppression that they bear, making them dream of a world that is reconciled and just, and inspiring them to struggle to bring it about. Finally, the Spirit is the creative power of difference and communion across differences. The Spirit is the one who stirs up the most diverse gifts within people and the widest range of services and ministries in communities, as the epistles to the Romans (12) and Corinthians (12) teach us. But this diversity does not fall into inequality and discrimination. We all drink of the same Spirit (1 Cor 12:13). The gifts are not given for self-promotion but for the good of the community (1 Cor 12:7).

The Spirit has been poured forth over us and dwells in the hearts of people, granting them enthusiasm, courage, and determination. It consoles the afflicted, keeps utopia alive in human minds and in the social imagination—the utopia of a fully redeemed humankind—and gives strength to anticipate it, even through revolutions in history. The Spirit is a divine Person together with the Son and the Father, emerging simultaneously with them and being essentially united to them through love, communion, and the divine life itself.

In the Bible the Spirit is like a whirlwind, a transforming force that, like love, is stronger than death. The Spirit is not, as it is for our culture, something evanescent and undefinable. How much drive would there be in our spirituality if we were to accept the Spirit as vital and ever-innovating energy!

✑

45. The Spirit is always united with the Son and the Father

How is the Holy Spirit, the third divine Person, related to the Father and the Son? The New Testament provides two pieces of information: It says that Jesus sends him from the Father (Jn 15:26), and it also says that the Spirit proceeds from the Father (Jn 15:26). How should the connection of the Spirit to the Father and Son be understood? This question has divided the church to the point that in 1054 it led to a split between the Roman Catholic Church and the Orthodox Catholic Church that has lasted to our own day. Underlying the different interpretations are different visions of God, church, and society. The Greeks, as we have already noted, start with the Father as source and supreme cause of the entire divinity. The Father pronounces his Word (Son) and together with it there emerges simultaneously the breath (Holy Spirit). Although the source is the same (the Father), Word and Breath are distinct. They also proceed differently from the Father, and hence the Father does not have two sons but an only begotten Son and one sole Spirit.

The Latins start from the single divine nature, which is the same in each of the Persons. In generating the Son, the Father entrusts everything to him (see Jn 16:15), including the ability to jointly spirate the Holy Spirit. Through communion, Father and Son are one (see Jn 10:30) and a single principle of spiration of the Holy Spirit. Otherwise, the Father would have two sons or there would be two causes of the Holy Spirit. Hence, the Latins say that the Spirit proceeds from the Father and the Son (*Filioque*) as from a single principle.

The Greeks reject this understanding of the Latins because they say that it sacrifices the specific feature of the Father; that of being the single cause and source of all divinity. The Son would also share in this exclusive quality (he would be a kind of second Father) and thus it would cease being exclusive. Both approaches have the same intention: to assure the full divinity and equality of the Persons of the Son and of the Holy Spirit. The Greeks reach this understanding by making the Son and Holy Spirit proceed from one and the same source, the Father. The Latins seek the same thing by another route, insisting that the three divine Persons are consubstantial, that is, that they are together in having the same nature. The Holy Spirit has the same nature that the Son has received from the Father. As the Son received from the Father, he has also, together with the Father, given to the Holy Spirit. Hence, say the Latins, the Holy Spirit proceeds from the Father and from the Son.

What is important ultimately is that we affirm that the Spirit is God, like the Father and the Son—as we pray in the creed that he "is equally adored and glorified and has spoken through the prophets."

In their face-to-face encounter, Father and Son allow dialogue to open up to perfect love. Love is perfect when they both, Father and Son, unite so that together they may love a Third. The Holy Spirit is this third Person, who represents the newness, openness, and absolute communion.

Here lies the importance of our own believing that the Father and the Son together, or the Father through the Son, "spirate" the Holy Spirit; namely, the fundamental importance of moving beyond the face to face toward convergence on a Third.

✌

46. The simultaneity of the Holy Spirit with the Father and the Son

Discussions about how the Holy Spirit proceeds and how he is related to the Father and the Son have divided the one church into two expressions in history: the Roman Catholic Church and the Orthodox Catholic Church. At two ecumenical councils, Lyons (1274) and Florence (1439), formulas of agreement were attempted. At Lyons it was clearly said that the Spirit proceeds from the Father and the Son, not as two principles and causes, but as a single principle. Father and Son are so united because they have the same communion-nature and the same life, so that they constitute a single source. At Florence it was explained that it can also be said that the Father spirates the Holy Spirit through the Son or by the Son. The Son is not, as it were, an instrumental cause, but through the same communion of love, he participates in the origin of the Holy Spirit. The explanations did not succeed in overcoming mutual suspicions of heresy, and the disputes continue to this day.

Meanwhile, theologians have deepened their understanding significantly. It is questioned whether the terminology employed—cause, procession, spiration—is adequate. The Holy Spirit seems to come third and to be subordinated to the Father or to the Father and the Son. Actually, there is no subordination in the Blessed Trinity, because the three Divine Ones are co-eternal, co-infinite, and coequal. "Before and after," "above and below" cannot be applied to them. We must start from where the New Testament starts, from the three Persons—from the Father, the Son, and the Holy Spirit, ever in relation and in communion. They are simultaneous, and they always come together. To avoid misunderstandings, rather than speaking of *cause*, *principle*, and *processions*, we would do better to speak of mutual revelation and acknowledgment. Each person is always related to the other two, because through perichoresis (interpenetration) each bears the others in itself. Each person is determined and is distinguished by the relationship that it establishes toward the other two. So we say: the Holy Spirit reveals the self-surrender of Father and Son. This love is the Holy Spirit. The Spirit recognizes the Father in the Son. The Spirit sees the Son as supreme expression of the Father. The Spirit is the joy of the relationship of intelligence and love between Father and Son. If we want to maintain the official terminology, we can also say that the Father "generates" the Son with the participation of the Holy Spirit, and "spirates" the Holy Spirit with the participation of the Son. The Holy Spirit together with the Son witnesses to the inaccessibility of the Father, and so they also share in eternity, because everything circulates among the divine Persons in an ebb and flow of eternal life and vital love.

The intention of Christians to create an egalitarian society,
built on mechanisms of participation by all and respectful of
differences, while keeping them from becoming inequalities,
is grounded in the equal dignity of the three divine Persons,
in their simultaneity, and in their loving shared existence.

✍

47. The feminine dimension of the Holy Spirit

Theological reflection saw the feminine dimensions in the Holy Spirit very early, more so than with reference to the Father and the Son—beginning with the name Holy Spirit, which in Hebrew is feminine. In the scriptures the Spirit is always associated with the function of generation and with the mystery of life. St. John's gospel delineates the activity of the Holy Spirit in characteristically feminine terminology. The Spirit consoles us as Paraclete, exhorts and teaches (Jn 14:26, 16:13) as mothers do with their little children; does not leave us orphans (Jn 14:18); teaches us to stammer the true name of God, *Abba*; and passes on to us the secret name of Jesus, which is Lord (1 Cor 12:3). Finally, as mothers also do, the Spirit educates us in prayer and in the way to ask for the right things (Rom 8:26).

In the Hebrew scriptures the Spirit also is associated with feminine functions. The very hovering of the Spirit over the waters of the primitive chaos of creation before the arrival of order seems to symbolize, according to interpreters, the incubation entailed in any kind of life. In the wisdom literature, as is widely known, Wisdom is loved as a woman (Sir 14:20-27) and is presented as wife and mother (Sir 15:2), sometimes identified with the Spirit (Wis 9:17). In some representations of the Trinity, the Holy Spirit is placed between the Father and the Son in the form of a woman. In the Odes of Solomon, a text from Syrian Christianity, the dove at the baptism of Jesus, which is one of the representations of the Holy Spirit, is called Mother. Some church fathers have called the Holy Spirit the divine Mother of the man Jesus, because the conception in the womb of the Virgin Mary took place by the work and grace of the Spirit (Mt 1:18). Macarius, a

great Christian theologian in Syria (d. 334), left this beauti
ful text: "The Spirit is our Mother because the Paraclete,
the Consoler, is ready to console us as a mother consoles her
child and because the faithful are reborn from him and so
they are children of this mysterious Mother, who is the Holy
Spirit." Indeed, the Spirit is present in the initial creation; it
is likewise active in the new creation, coming down upon
Mary and causing her to conceive the incarnate Son; it descends upon Jesus in baptism and sends him out on mission;
it raises Jesus from among the dead (Acts 13:33; Rom 1:4);
and it descends on the apostles and so launches the missionary church. In the body of Christ which is the church, the
Spirit as Mother conceives new brothers and sisters of Jesus
and fills Christian communities with life through charisms
and services. To say it again, the Spirit has feminine and masculine dimensions, but it is beyond sex. The values that we
discover in the feminine, which is present in woman and in
man, encounter in the Holy Spirit one of their eternal sources.

*God finds us in values that our culture calls masculine, such
as strength, determination, work, a masculine that exists in
both man and woman. But God also finds us in feminine
values, which also exist in both sexes, such as tenderness,
the sense of mystery, and care. The Holy Spirit in its action
among us has privileged that side of human existence.*

⌀

48. Mission of the Holy Spirit:
To unify and create the new

The action of the Holy Spirit in history is a reflection of its
action within the Trinity, where the Spirit is the principle of

diversity and of union between those who are distinct (Father and Son). Hence the Spirit is love and communion par excellence, even though each divine Person is communion and love. Whenever in history we encounter driving forces that build up love, that conciliate where differences live together in harmony, there we discern the ineffable presence of the Holy Spirit's action. The Spirit is linked to transforming and innovating action. The Spirit's action permeates human acts, making them bring about the design of the Trinity. In particular, actors in history, charismatic leaders, those who provide new horizons, those who clear new paths, are expressions of the power of the Holy Spirit. More particularly, when the poor resist oppression, when they organize to seek life, bread, and freedom, when in the midst of struggle they maintain faith and tenderness toward others, they are the great historic sacraments of the active presence of the Holy Spirit.

The Holy Spirit is linked to the new and the alternative. We always have to deal with laws, habits, and institutions; they give us security and assure us a direction. But the human spirit is always open upward and forward—it is insatiable. From time to time identity crises occur; the stars in our sky go dark. Societies feel that new paths are needed. Revolutions occur and leave behind venerable institutions and well-worn paths. New paths open up; a new order is created. The Holy Spirit is always present in these usually painful processes of structural change. It is the Spirit who inaugurates the new heaven and new earth. Figuratively, we could say that the Holy Spirit is the creative imagination of God. The Spirit is at work particularly in the church, because it is the sacrament of the Spirit of Jesus. Alongside the legitimate structure of power there is charism, which comes from the Spirit. The Holy Spirit makes present the message of Jesus and does not let the spirit of authoritarianism prevail in the community, or ritualism dominate in celebrations, or Christian thinking fall into boring repetition of formulas. The saving efficacy of the Spirit is evidenced in the sacraments, particularly in the eucharist. The Spirit comes as a grace that divinizes our life; through the Spirit's activity the words of Christ who instituted the sacrament of the eucharist, become effective and bring the sacred humanity of Christ into our midst, under the form of bread and wine.

Where would society and the churches be without the emergence of innovators, creative people, who have new ideas, invent new rhythms, and discover new paths for education, agriculture, politics, and religion? It is through these twists and folds in the social fabric that the Holy Spirit, creator and giver of life, is made manifest.

❧

49. The unique relationship between the Holy Spirit and Mary

The Holy Spirit, together with the Son, has been sent to earth to sanctify all creatures and lead them back to the bosom of the Trinity. Who has welcomed the coming of the Holy Spirit? To whom has the Spirit come personally in full self-giving? Theological reflection to this day has not been entirely precise on this point. We do know that the Spirit is in the life of all the poor and all the just in history, is present more intensely in the community of the faithful, acts particularly in the sacraments, and provides infallible assistance to the pope when he addresses the entire church to express the faith in a consciously binding way for all the faithful. But could we not specify better the personal presence of the

Spirit in time, as we do with regard to the Son? The Son was received by the sacred humanity of Jesus; this is the essence of the mystery of the incarnation, the union, without separation or confusion, between the human reality and the divine reality in Jesus of Nazareth, Son of God and our brother in the flesh. Could we not find something similar with regard to the Holy Spirit? Indeed, it is possible for Christians to elaborate respectfully a hypothesis (theologoumenon) that does not offend the other truths of the faith and that advances our knowledge of the love of the Blessed Trinity. This is not an official doctrine that could be taught in catechism classes. It is an effort marked by piety and respect to peer more deeply into the mysteries of God, which ever challenge us and invite us to delve more deeply. We are going to set forth such a theological hypothesis.

We find illuminating a text in St. Luke that says of Mary: "The Holy Spirit will come upon you, and the power of the Most High will overshadow you; therefore the child to be born will be . . . called Son of God" (1:35). It is said here that the Spirit must come down upon Mary, as indeed happened. "To overshadow" is the biblical way of saying that the Spirit pitches its tent in Mary; that is, that it has there a palpable presence (cf. Ex 40:34-35). Vatican II calls Mary "sacrament of the Holy Spirit" (*Lumen Gentium*, no. 53). The presence of the Spirit in Mary makes her mother; it transforms her human motherhood into divine motherhood. That is why the one born of her is "Son of God." The council says that Mary is, as it were, "fashioned by the Holy Spirit into a kind of new substance and new creature" (*Lumen Gentium*, no. 56). To say that she is "fashioned by the Holy Spirit" implies recognizing a unique relationship with the third Person of the Blessed Trinity. Here the dignity of woman reaches its highest peak, similar to what takes place with man in Jesus. Woman and man are image and likeness of God, of the Blessed Trinity (Gn 1:27). Both share in the divinity, each in its own manner, but really and truly. We, brothers and sisters of Jesus and Mary, will share in union with them, each of us in our own proper way.

> *The masculine in Jesus was divinized by the incarnation of the Son. And the feminine? Did it not have equal dignity? Together with the masculine is not the feminine also image and likeness of the triune God? It is well to maintain the balance sought by God and to divinize the feminine as well. Cannot Mary be seen as she in whom the Holy Spirit dwells and elevates the feminine to the divine?*

の

❧ X ❧

The Trinity in heaven
and the Trinity on earth:
The internal history of the Trinity
reflected in the external history
of creation

50. *As it was in the beginning: The eternity of the Trinity*

We are in time. The future comes, passes through the present, and becomes past. Or we come from the past, pass through the present, and head toward the future. We all have a beginning, a middle, and an end. We find ourselves within a limited stretch of time. That is not the way it is with the Blessed Trinity. It is eternal; it has no beginning, nor will it have an end. We stand here before a boundless mystery. It surpasses our thinking and our imagination. How shed some light on this mystery? Perhaps we succeed only negatively, that is, by saying what eternity is not; what it is utterly escapes us. But that is no reason to fall silent; even if there are no concepts, there are at least some hints.

The Blessed Trinity never began. It always existed, from the beginning and eternally; it will never cease to exist! Here emerges the limit of our understanding: how do we represent someone who has always existed? Our experience tells us that everything we know begins one day, develops, and then dies. Or in the case of persons, begins one day and then goes on to endless eternity. With the Blessed Trinity there is no beginning and there will be no end. What causes us problems is not so much the "no end" but the "no beginning." Hence, eternity does not mean a quantity but seeks to express a divine quality. The Blessed Trinity is so perfect, it has life so fully and simultaneously, that it does not present any insufficiency. To be open and in communion is perfection. If it brings into its perichoretic communion other persons and even the entire universe, that is not out of any lack but out of superabundance. It infinitely expands and is expressed, and at each moment it is absolute and completely full.

When we say that the Trinity exists without beginning, we seek to confess the following: Before the least bit of atomic material existed, before any sign of life emerged, before the ages began to pass, the Father already existed, totally expressing himself in the Son, and together infinitely loving the Holy Spirit. We as creatures were in the divine mind as a plan to be carried out at a particular moment, and thus we would be able to participate in trinitarian communion. We do not understand what we are saying. We merely seek to affirm that love, communion, the loving interweaving of the divine Persons is something so marvelous and complete that has always existed and will exist forever.

Eternity is a problem only when we want to understand it—and we are never going to understand it. But it becomes a source of joy when we know and believe that we are going

*to share it in an endless celebration—in a full, shared life of
brothers and sisters and friends, in a dazzling victory over
time without the least shadow of bitterness.*

∽

51. The Trinity in heaven manifests itself on earth

The Trinity reveals itself as it is: communion of the Father, the Son, and the Holy Spirit. The apostles and the early Christians discovered that God the Father was present and acting in creation and history. They recognized that in Jesus of Nazareth the very Son of God was incarnate. They saw that the Holy Spirit was acting in history and in the community, moving people's hearts so that they would acknowledge God as Father, accept Jesus as the Son of God—the Son who saved us with his life, commitment to justice, and limitless love, and by his death and resurrection—and see that he was continuing to permeate history in order to bring it to its happy conclusion. They called these three presences God, without thereby falling into polytheism or betraying faith in one God. From now on God was going to be understood as Trinity, that is, as communion of Father, Son, and Holy Spirit, while being one sole God of love, life, and communication.

This historic experience makes it possible to say that if we recognize that three persons exist under the name of "God," it is because God is inherently triune and is the communion of three Persons. The three Persons do not constitute realities just for our perception—it is a reality in itself. The Trinity on earth corresponds to the Trinity in heaven. We can also say the reverse: The Trinity in heaven corresponds to the Trinity on earth.

This statement can be grounded better if we start from the mystery of the coming of the Son to the humanity of Jesus of Nazareth and of the descent of the Spirit on the Virgin Mary, as attested by St. Luke (1:35). The Son is really present in Jesus, so much so that we say that his concrete humanity here is the humanity of God. The Holy Spirit is so present in the Virgin Mary (according to our understanding) that the Spirit acts on her maternal potency, making her to be Mother of God. The one who is born of her will be Son of God (Lk 1:35). The Spirit and the Son are among us. Both, however, point back to the Father. The incarnate Son continually confesses that he has been sent by the Father. The Spirit is also sent by the Father at the request of the Son. Hence we have here the presence of the entire Trinity in our life. This is a sign that the Trinity is not our creation; it exists in itself. The ultimate reality of creation is communion of three Divine Ones. We are surrounded by them, invited to share in their life, enter into their communion, and belong to the reign of the Trinity.

We do not deceive ourselves nor are we deceived by what is most important in the universe. What is behind everything? What sustains and permeates all beings? Where does the desire of our heart point? It is the communion of the Diverse Ones, it is the love that unifies all, it is the Father, the Son, and the Holy Spirit, ever joined among themselves and ever joined with us.

✍

52. The glory and joy of the Trinity

Through the incarnation of the Son in Jesus and through the coming of the Spirit upon Mary, there is a history of the

Blessed Trinity within our own history. This history is not characterized by the visible dimensions of grandeur, glory, and power. The path privileged by God in Hebrew and Christian scriptures, and in the religions of the world, is that of simplicity and humility. Jesus was a poor man, an itinerant prophet, utterly powerless except for the power that flowed from the word and from radical goodness. Mary was a woman of the people who journeyed in the darkness of faith and shared in the constraints of the historic situation of her Son. Yet they were the living presence of the Son and the Holy Spirit in our midst. Even in these humble situations they showed what the Son and the Holy Spirit in the Trinity are. Jesus revealed the merciful face of the Father by being merciful to the sinners he encountered. He manifested the divine truth against all distortions of the religion of that time, a truth that liberates the human, that lightens the load of traditions, and that places the accent on the fundamental calling of each person to loving-kindness, forgiveness, and service of others, even when out of fidelity to this truth he had to accept death. Likewise, the Holy Spirit is the power of resistance, union among all, courage in difficulty, liberation from oppression. Mary followed her Son in the same fate, helped the community united at Pentecost, adhered to the mysterious will of the Father at the foot of her Son's cross, and had the audacity to ask for the intervention of the God who liberates the poor to change power relationships here on earth (see Lk 1:51-53). In other words, the Blessed Trinity is present in history through the Father, who sends the Son and the Holy Spirit, who, through their specific coming in Jesus and Mary, have taken on the human condition, subject to the common ailments of mortal existence and marked by the consequences of sin. They have liberated from within.

However, it is the role of faith not simply to glimpse some light about the interior life of the three divine Persons in themselves, but also to perceive the infinite joy that permeates trinitarian relations. They are three distinct gazes constituting a single vision of love. It is the wedding of the Three in a single communion of life. The interweaving of the divine Three, in an ebb and flow of self-giving, impels the ecstasy of intimacy and of embrace, and the swelling of tenderness. It is unending happiness in a boundless ocean of fulfillment, in an ecstatic mutual fascination, in an eternally full life. It is the glory and joy of the Father, the Son, and the Holy Spirit, ineffably together.

Union of diversity—behold the essence of the mystery of the Trinity—is not simply the intellectual expression of faith in God-communion, but it constitutes a source of subjective fulfillment, the outpouring of joy, and the experience of beauty and also of pleasure and good feeling.

❧

53. Creation projected toward communion

In God's innermost mystery, God is not solitude but communion of three divine Persons. This communion among Father, Son, and Holy Spirit is by its very nature expansive; it unfolds in myriad ways.

The Trinity desired companions in this eternal communion. The secret meaning of all creation lies precisely here: being different from God so as to be brought into God; being different from the Trinity in order to be included within the communion of the Trinity.

Creation is not necessary in the sense of being imposed on God. It derives from the freedom and love of the three divine Persons in wanting an expansion of their communion on another level, different from the internal level on which they live together infinitely, the temporal and finite level. The divine Three participate in this creation. They always act together as a single principle of being, life, and love. As St. Augustine put it, the world was made by the Father, through the Son, in the Holy Spirit. Each Person stamps creation with something of its own specific property. That is why creation is so rich, because behind it and within it is hidden the wealth of each divine Person, as that Person is, ever distinct and ever in communion. That is also why creation is pervaded, within the most variegated differences, by a drive toward union, convergence, and communion that mirrors the internal reality of the Trinity.

Creation has two faces: one temporal and visible, the one we see in the succession of all the forms and expressions of being; the other eternal and invisible as idea and project of the three divine Persons. The possibility of creation comes out of the inner depth of trinitarian communion. The Father, united to the Holy Spirit, reveals himself totally in the Son and to the Son. The eternal image of the Father together with the Spirit is the Son. But in the Son the Father also projects all possible lesser images of himself; they are all the creatures who constitute the universe. As a projection of the Father with the love of the Holy Spirit, creation is eternal, and hence it is situated within the circle of trinitarian communion. Insofar as, from among the infinity of the images of the Trinity, the divine Three choose some to exist outside of this circle of inner communion, the creation as we now have it emerges. What was an eternal intention or project now becomes a temporal project; what was projection is now reality—as reality it is drawn from nothing by the Trinity. It is different from the Trinity, but it is stamped with the marks of the Trinity. Because it is different, it can receive within itself the personal communication of each of the Persons; it can be assumed within the trinitarian communion. It is for this that we exist; it is for this that everything existing exists.

The ultimate root of our history is found in the inner history of the Trinity, the play of mutual relations among the divine Three, eternally producing diversity and unification.

❦

54. Each divine Person helps in creating the universe

In the Trinity everything is trinitarian, that is, everything circulates, everything always includes the three divine Persons, everything is expression of the communion of the three divine Distinct Ones. This is also true of creation. St. Thomas Aquinas, in the *Summa Theologica*, says that each Person acts in its own fashion, and they always act together (as a single principle) in the creation of the universe. He says it is like an artist, who applies intelligence and love in producing the work of art. It is similar with the Father who fashions creation, with the Intelligence that is his Son, and with Love, which is the Holy Spirit. Hence, all things point back to their Creator, all reveal and entail an extremely logical wisdom, all are lovable and expression of a possible love. In short, all beings are image and likeness of the Trinity. Let us look a little at how we can imagine this intimate collaboration of the three Persons in the creation of all beings. The Father acts as boundless mystery, as the one in whom we see that the Trinity is eternal, without beginning and giving everything its beginning. All things have their mysterious character; no matter how much we know them, we can always know more; they all point to a higher cause whence they come. This is the mystery of the Father, who is there proclaimed. Furthermore, each thing causes something else to derive from it. It is begun, but at the same time it becomes the created beginning of something else. This is yet another expression of the Father, who is without beginning and lies at the beginning of everything. Everything is fatherly and motherly.

The Son is revelation and intelligence. Every creature reveals something of God. It shows the presence of a supreme wisdom. The structure of each being is such that it ever reveals itself, shows its truth, and in this manner enters into communication with the other. Such characteristics denote the presence of the Son within creation. Hence, all things are brotherly and sisterly, are brothers and sisters to each other.

The Spirit is love and union. The communion that characterizes the inner divine mystery becomes visible in the Spirit. The things of the universe are not simply thrown together, but they make up totalities of meaning; there is order, despite the apparent chaos. Particularly among persons, love and attraction to union and communion are at work. In these cosmic and vital energies there emerge signs of the presence of the Holy Spirit. Creatures always make a spiritual appeal that comes from the divine Spirit.

Every creature and the whole of creation bear the action of these three divine Energies. They are not blind energies, but the activities of Persons, distinct but in communion, imparting depth, light, and warmth to the universe.

Each existing being bears the mark of the Father and hence always appears as a mystery; bears the mark of the Son and

hence can be understood as—and is—brotherly and sisterly;
bears the mark of the Holy Spirit and hence can be loved
and nourishes our spiritual dimension.

༺༒

55. Signs of the Trinity under the shadow of history

The cosmos and human life have a trinitarian structure.
This corresponds to the order of creation and also to the
order of grace. We can and we must live this dimension consciously. In the present, however, we do not feel the joy and
happiness that this truth signifies. We are groping our way
in the light of faith, imbued with hope and building up love.
The signs of the Trinity occur in the obscurity of the mind.
We believe without being able to see adequately what we
believe. The presence of the divine Persons in the historico-
social process is especially murky. This process contains con-
flicts and contradictions, and sin, which also does its in-
sidious work of breaking apart the communion desired by
the Trinity. It is in this area that we must believe and not
allow ourselves to be led solely by what is evident to the
senses. Faith transcends what is merely visible and peers
down deeply to where things are linked to the mystery of
God.

In faith we see that the struggle of the oppressed against
the sin of hunger and violence has a particularly trinitarian
intensity. Whenever things start over from the beginning, after every failure—or even after what was sought has been ob-
tained—it is a sign of the Father that such an undertaking is
announced. Whenever in the midst of contradictions progress
is being made toward more life-enhancing relationships of

greater sister-and-brotherhood, it is the Son who is there revealing himself. The union of the oppressed, the convergence of interests toward the good of all, courage to face obstacles, the fearlessness of the denunciatory word, the ability to create alternatives, solidarity with the most oppressed among the oppressed to the point of being identified with their cause and life—these are hints of the active presence of the Spirit in history.

History is human; clashes and convergences take place side by side. It has meaning, and meanings are created within it alongside the persistence of existential and collective absurdities. Even so, it is mysteriously inhabited by the august mystery of the Father, the Son, and the Holy Spirit. This presence is effective, providing encouragement for the struggle, capacity to resist the power of sin, creative spirit, and a will to transform history. This history is the theater of the possible glory of the Trinity, present in time under shadows and crosses, at the end of time in the form of full openness and unending celebration. The universe is pregnant with the mystery of the most holy Trinity, so close that we do not perceive it, so transcendent that it overflows us on all sides, so intimate that it dwells in the depths of our hearts, so real that it persists, despite sin and all its perverse consequences.

> *It is wrong and offensive to God to say that the Blessed Trinity is a mystery so deep that it leaves no sign in creation and in human life. It is a sign of either weak faith or complete religious inattention to fail to perceive the communion, wealth of diversity, and unity among all things.*

✑

56. Now and forever: The Trinity in creation and creation in the Trinity

Creation exists in order to welcome the Trinity into itself. The Trinity seeks to welcome creation within itself. Stated in a brief formula: The Trinity in creation seeks to bring creation into the Trinity. Will there be a moment in history when the reality of God will be manifested as it is and can be grasped within the limits of the human creature? Yes, there will. We have already had its anticipation with the incarnation of the Son and the coming of the Holy Spirit over Mary and the community of Jesus' followers. In other words, a portion of our history has become history of the Trinity. Now history in its entirety is to become history of the Trinity. Then there will be no more reading of signs but the joy of direct and transparent presence. The universe, after the millions and millions of years of its rise, after the unfolding of its latent potentialities, at last, overt, after the cosmic crisis by which it has been purified of all evil, will finally attain the reign of the Trinity. Through the transforming power of the Spirit and through the liberating action of the Son, the universe ultimately will arrive at the Father. Now begins the true history of creation with its trinitarian Creator. The mystery of creation stands facing the mystery of the Father. Every creature will be facing its eternal prototype, the Father's Son. The communion and union existing among all will be revealed as an expression of the Holy Spirit. Creation will forever be united to the mystery of life, love, and communion of the Father, the Son, and the Holy Spirit. Men will find themselves assumed in the likeness of Jesus of Nazareth by the Person of the eternal

Son. Now they will eternally be adoptive sons in the eternal Son, expression of the love, wisdom, and life of the Father. Women will see themselves assumed—in accordance with our theological theory—in the likeness of Mary of Nazareth, by the Holy Spirit. Thus divinized, men and women will reveal the motherly and fatherly face of God in communion, now including the Trinity with creation and creation with the Trinity.

It is the feast of the redeemed; it is the heavenly dance of those set free. It is the shared life of the sons and daughters in the home and homeland of the Trinity as the Father, the Son, and the Holy Spirit.

In creation thus made trinitarian we will pray and give praise. We will praise and love each of the divine Persons and the communion among them all. We will be invited by them to love and praise, to play and sing, to dance and adore, forever and ever, Amen. Finally, the true history of the Trinity in creation and of creation in the Trinity will unfold. What was outside will be brought inside; what was inside will be communicated outward. Outside and inside will be in never-ending communion, communion that is the mystery of the Trinity itself.

This entire universe, these stars above our head, these forests, these birds, these insects, these rivers, and these stones, everything, everything, is going to be preserved, transfigured, and made temple of the Blessed Trinity. And we will live in a grand house, as in a single family, minerals, vegetables, animals, and humans with the Father, the Son, and the Holy Spirit. Amen.

Conclusion

Summary of trinitarian doctrine: The whole in many fragments

1. When we say "God" we must always implicitly understand the Blessed Trinity. The Trinity is the Father, the Son, and the Holy Spirit, always together and in perfect communion. Because of this perfect communion the three divine Persons are one sole God-of-life-and-love.

2. It is dangerous for us to insist on the statement that there is one God, apart from a trinitarian faith. Some religious and political leaders invoke this single-focus understanding of God to justify their authoritarianism and exclusionary attitude and practice.

3. What makes it possible to catch a glimpse of why the three divine Persons are one God is *perichoresis*. Perichoresis signifies the eternal interrelating that exists among the divine Three. Each person lives from the other, with the other, through the other, and for the other Person. From all eternity they are interwoven and interpenetrated, so that we cannot think or speak of one Person, such as the Father, without having to also think and speak of the Son and the Holy Spirit.

4. We only know the Trinity in itself through the signs that it has left us in history, in human life, in religions, and in the Bible. In the journey of Jesus and in the action of the Holy Spirit in the early Christians, it is clear that there is God the Father, God the Son, and God the Holy Spirit, ever together and in eternal mutual communion.

5. The fundamental challenge of trinitarian faith is as follows: How do we equate three with one and one with three? How reach the unity of a single God from the Trinity of Persons? And how move from the unity of a single God to the Trinity of Persons?

6. The church expresses its official doctrine as follows: God is one *nature* in three *Persons*. Nature has to do with the unity of the Trinity. Person guarantees the Trinity in unity. There are two *processions*, that is, the manner in which one person proceeds from the other. The Father generates the Son (first procession), and likewise the Father together with the Son spirates the Holy Spirit (second procession). There are also the *relations*, that is, the connections among the three Persons: paternity, filiation, active spiration, and passive spiration; through the relations the Persons are distinguished from one another; they are also distinguished by their specific personality. Finally, there are the *missions* of the Son to liberate us and make us sons and daughters, and that of the Holy Spirit to sanctify us and lead us back to the bosom of the Blessed Trinity.

7. There are three ways of rationally delving into trinitarian doctrine: the Orthodox, Latin, and modern approaches. *Orthodox theology* (of the Eastern Orthodox Church) starts with the unity of nature of the Father. The Father is source and origin of the entire divinity. Through

his mouth he speaks forth the Word, which is the Son. As his Word is emitted, the Breath, which is the Holy Spirit, simultaneously comes from him. The three receive from the Father the entire divine nature, and so they are consubstantial. *Latin theology* (of the Roman Catholic Church) starts with the divine nature, which is spiritual. The absolute Spirit without principle and origin of all is the Father. The Father knows himself through his Intelligence and generates the Son. Father and Son love one another and both spirate the Holy Spirit. The same nature is found in all three, and hence they are a single God. *Modern theology* starts with the three Persons together. It highlights the fact that the three are ever interrelated and in eternal communion (perichoresis). This relation is so absolute that the divine Three are united without being merged, and are thus a single living God.

8. There are three erroneous ways of conceiving faith in the Trinity: tritheism, subordinationism, and modalism. In *tritheism* it is said that there are three gods: the Father, the Son, and the Holy Spirit. Such a vision does not consider perichoresis, namely, the eternal interrelating among the divine Three. *Subordinationism* regards only the Father as true God. The Son and the Holy Spirit are subordinated to him and do not have the same divine nature; the divine equality among the three Persons is thereby divided. *Modalism* affirms that there is only one God but three modes of his manifestation in the world. When the one God creates, he uses the mask of Father; when he liberates, the pseudonym of Son; and when he sanctifies and brings everything back to the reign, he is presented with the face of the Holy Spirit; in such a vision the Trinity of Persons is abandoned.

9. All the technical expressions that we use to try to understand something of the Trinity—*generation* by the Father

toward the Son, or *spiration* by the Father and the Son toward the Holy Spirit, or the other words such as *nature, person, relations, processions,* or *missions*—have an approximating, analogous, and figurative value, We can also use the biblical manner of expressions such as *revelation, recognition, communion, life,* and *love.*

10.   Reason is not the only way into the heart of the Trinity. There is also the imagination. Through it we grasp better the existential meaning that the Blessed Trinity has for our life. It is through our imagination that we realize that the human person, the family, community, society, church, and cosmos are signs, symbols, and sacraments of the Trinity.

11.   By virtue of the interrelating (perichoresis) among the three divine Persons, everything in them is threefold and shared. This does not mean that there cannot be actions proper to each of the Persons through which what is proper to each particular Person appears.

12.   The proper action of the Father is to project all creation in the act of "generating" the Son in the light of the Holy Spirit. Hence all beings have a character of mystery (which comes from the Father) and also a filial nature (which comes from the Son, generated by the Father), and a spiritual sense as well (full of drive, which comes from the Holy Spirit).

13.   The proper action of the Son is the full communication of revelation and the incarnation. Through this communication he frees us from our inhumanity and divinizes us, making us sons and daughters of God.

14.   The proper action of the Holy Spirit is to unify and to create what is new through sanctification. The Spirit has done this fully in Jesus and in a personal manner in most holy Mary.

15.   The ultimate meaning of creation is its capacity for being a receptacle of the communication of the three divine Persons. Trinitarian communion is opened out and invites creation, persons, and all creatures to participate in its life of communion. Creation will be, at the end of history, the body of the Trinity.

16.   Communion, which is the nature of the Trinity, means a critique of all kinds of exclusion and nonparticipation that exist and remain in society and also in the churches. It also encourages the changes needed for communion and participation to be present in all realms of social and religious life. The Blessed Trinity represents the best program for full liberation.

17.   The Blessed Trinity is a sacramental mystery. In other words, it is something that appears in many signs, that can always be more known; yet our effort to know never ends. Hence, even in eternity, living among the three divine Persons, we will never cease to grow in knowledge, ever open to discover new aspects, and our thirst for knowing, loving, touching, and sharing will never end.

Glossary

Technical theological terms used for discussion of the Trinity

Action ad extra (outward action): these are actions that the Trinity works outside the circle of the Trinity, such as the creation of the universe, revelation, the salvation of human beings.

Action ad intra (inward action): spoken of intra-trinitarian actions, within the trinitarian circle, such as the generation of the Son and the spiration of the Holy Spirit.

Anamnesis: literally "memorial"; the remembrance (after the consecration of the bread and wine) of the passion, resurrection, and ascension of Christ.

Anaphora: literally "offering"; the central part of the eucharistic celebration, including the consecration, anamnesis (remembrance of the passion, death, resurrection, and ascension of Christ), and communion

Apophatic: literally, "without word"; the stance of believers before the divine mystery; after saying all they can, they respectfully keep silence. There is said to be an apophatic theology that ends in the silence of veneration and adoration.

Appropriated action: an action attributed to one of the divine Persons, even though it is brought about by the Three together, because of an affinity with the properties of that Person. Thus creation is attributed to the Father, redemption to the Son, and sanctification to the Holy Spirit.

Arche (principle): Greek term to express the fact that the Father is principle, source, and unique cause in the generation of the Son and the spiration of the Holy Spirit.

Arianism: a heresy proposed by Arius (250-336), a priest in Alexandria in Egypt. Arius advocated subordinationism, by which the Son (and the Holy Spirit) would be subordinated to the Father. They would be sublime creatures, created before the universe, and hence would not be God. There is also adoptionist subordinationism: the Son is said to be adopted as Son, by the grace of the Father, but does not have the same nature as the Father.

Charism: "grace" in Greek; a gift or an ability that the Holy Spirit has given to a person for the sake of the good of all.

Circumincession: active interpenetration of the divine Persons among themselves because of the eternal communion between them. *See Perichoresis.*

Divine essence: that which constitutes the triune God in itself, the divinity; being, love, goodness, truth, and reciprocal communion in the form of the absolute and infinite. *See also* Divine nature; Substance.

Divine nature: the one sole divine substance in each of the Persons, which has to do with the unity or union in God.

Doxology: formula of praise (*doxa* in Greek). Generally comes at the end of prayers in which the Father is thanked through the Son in the unity of the Holy Spirit.

DS: abbreviation of the name of two theologians, Denzinger and Schönmetzer, who published the book *Enchiridion Symbolorum definitionum et declarionum de rebus fidei et morum,* which is a collection of the creeds, definitions, and declaration on matters of faith and morals that the magisterium of the church (councils, synods, and official pronouncements of the pope) has declared throughout the history of Christianity. The first edition appeared in 1854; it has been repeatedly revised and updated since then.

Economic Trinity: the Trinity as self-revealed in human history and as acting so that we might share in the trinitarian life.

Economy (of salvation): the various phases of the carrying out of God's project or plan in history or God's own gradual self-revelation; with regard to the Trinity, the economy means the order in procession starting with the Father: first comes the Son, and then the Holy Spirit.

Ek: Greek particle, corresponding to Latin *ex* or *de,* the proceeding of one divine Person from another. Thus the

Son is generated *from* (i.e., or *ex* or *de*) the Father; or the Holy Spirit proceeds *from the* Father and *from the* Son (according to Latin theology).

Ekporeusis: Greek term to designate the proceeding of the Holy Spirit from the Father, who is always Father of the Son. In Latin the term is "spiration."

Epiklesis: celebration in which the Holy Spirit is involved.

Essential affirmation: that affirmation which is based on the equal and unique divine essence in the three Persons. It is an essential affirmation, for example, to say, "God is merciful, infinite, eternal," meaning that the divine essence is eternal, infinite, and merciful.

Filioque: literally, "and from the Son"; doctrine according to which the Holy Spirit proceeds from the Father and from the Son as from a single principle. This doctrinal interpretation is also called filioque-ism; it is common among Latin theologians.

Gennesis: Greek term to express the generation of the Son by the Father.

Homoiousious: literally, "of similar nature"; heresy according to which the Son's nature was not equal but similar to that of the Father.

Homoousious: literally, "of the same and equal nature"; the Son and the Holy Spirit are said to have the very same nature as the Father. The Persons are consubstantial.

Hypostasis: Greek term to designate a divine Person. *See* Person; *Prosopon.*

Immanent Trinity: the Trinity considered in itself, in its eternity and perichoretic communion among the Father, the Son, and the Holy Spirit.

Innascibility: property solely of the Father, of not being generated or born or begun; the Father is principle without principle.

Kenosis: Greek expression for annihilation or emptying; it is the way chosen by the divine Persons (Son and Holy Spirit) for their self-communication in history; opposite of *doxa*, the mode of glory.

Koinonia: Greek expression for *communio* in Latin and "communion" in European languages; the proper way of relating to persons, including divine Persons.

Mission: in trinitarian theology the self-communication of the Person of the Son to the human nature of Jesus of Nazareth and of the Holy Spirit to the just, Mary, and the church; the enthronement of humankind in the bosom of the trinitarian mystery.

Modalism: heretical doctrine according to which the Trinity constitutes simply three human ways of seeing one and the same God, or three modes (masks) of one and the same God being made manifest to human beings; God is not understood as Trinity intrinsically but as one and unique.

Monarchianism: the negation of the Trinity for the sake of strict monotheism.

Monarchy: in trinitarian language the unique causality of the Father; it is the Father alone who generates the Son and spirates (as Father of the Son) the Holy Spirit; a characteristically Greek Orthodox expression.

Monotheism: the affirmation that there is only one God; the Old Testament is familiar with a pre-trinitarian monotheism, prior to the revelation of the Blessed Trinity; after the revelation of the mystery of the Trinity there can be an "a-trinitarian" monotheism: it speaks of God without taking the trinity of Persons into account, as though God were a single reality and existing only in God's substance; there also exists trinitarian monotheism: God is one and unique by virtue of the one sole substance existing in the Father, the Son, and the Holy Spirit, or by virtue of the eternal communion and perichoresis existing from the beginning among the three divine Persons.

Mystery: strictly speaking, the reality of the Blessed Trinity as inaccessible to human reason; even after it has been communicated, it can be known by the human mind indefinitely without ever being totally grasped; the triune God is mystery, not simply for the human mind but in itself, because the Trinity is essentially infinite and eternal; in salvation-history terms the triune God is a sacramental mystery, that is, a mystery that is communicated to us through the attitudes and words of Jesus and in the action of the Holy Spirit in ecclesial community and in human history.

Notion: the characteristics proper to each of the Persons, differentiating them from one another; paternity and innascibility for the Father; filiation for the Son; active spiration for the Father and the Son; passive spiration for the Holy Spirit; thus there are five notions.

Notional affirmation: that which is based only on the Persons in their distinction from one another. There are four notional affirmations: the Father generates; the Son is generated; the Father and the Son (or the Father through the Son) spirate the Holy Spirit; the Holy Spirit is spirated by the Father and the Son (or through the Son).

Patreque: literally, "and through the Father"; in the Trinity all relations are threefold; thus the Son is related to the Holy Spirit together with the Father or through the Father; likewise, the Holy Spirit loves the Son through the Father and together with the Father, and so forth.

Peghe (source): Greek expression to designate the Father as only and infinite *source* from which the Son and the Holy Spirit spring forth.

Perichoresis: Greek expression, literally meaning that a Person contains the other two (in a static sense) or that each of the Persons interpenetrates the others mutually (active sense); the adjective *perichoretic* is intended to designate the communion nature in effect among the divine Persons. *See* Circumincession.

Person: in trinitarian language, that which is distinct in God, the Father, the Son, and the Holy Spirit; the individuality of each Person who simultaneously exists in itself and in eternal communion with the other two. *See Hypostasis*; Subsistence.

Procession: derivation of one Person out of the other, but consubstantially, in the unity of a single nature, substance, essence, or divinity.

Proper action: a specific action of a particular divine Person, such as the incarnation of the Son or the coming of the Holy Spirit upon Mary when Jesus was conceived.

Prosopon: literally "mask," "face"; in trinitarian language, a Greek word to designate the divine Person in its individuality; synonymous with *hypostasis*. *See* Person.

Relation: in trinitarian language, the ordering of a Person to the others, or the eternal communion among the divine Three; there are four relations: paternity, filiation, active spiration, and passive spiration.

Relational gestalt: term used by the German theologian J. Moltmann to express the contribution of the Son in the spiration of the Holy Spirit together with the Father; the Person of the Spirit comes from the Father; the concrete configuration (Gestalt) of the Person of the Holy Spirit is derived from the Son. It is relational because the Persons are always turned toward one another and within one another.

Sabelianism: heresy of Sabelius (early third century in Rome) also called modalism: the Son and the Holy Spirit are understood to be merely modes of the divinity and not distinct Persons. *See* Modalism.

Spiration: act by which the Father together with the Son makes the Person of the Holy Spirit proceed (according to the Latins) as from a single principle. The Greeks have the Spirit derive only from the Father of the Son or from the Father through the Son.

Spirituque: literally, "and of the Holy Spirit"; inasmuch as relations in the Trinity are always ternary, the Father is said to generate the Son together with the Holy Spirit, or the Son is said to recognize the Father together with the Holy Spirit, and so forth.

Subordinationism: the heresy of Arius, according to which the Son and the Holy Spirit are said to be subordinate, in an unequal relationship to the Father, and do not have the very same form and very same nature; or they are said to be exalted creatures, but merely adopted by the Father into his divinity (adoptionism).

Subsistence: one of the synonyms for Person or hypostasis; inasmuch as there is nothing accidental in the Trinity, the relations among the Persons are said to be subsistent relations; the Person is considered to be a subsistent relation.

Substance: in trinitarian language, that which unites in God and is identical in each one of the Persons. *See* Divine Nature; Divine Essence.

Symbol: technical term in early theology for the formulas by which the church officially summarized its faith; synonym of *creed.*

Theogony: process giving rise to a divinity or explanation of the mystery of the Trinity in such a way as to give the impression that the Persons are not co-eternal and coequal but that some are produced from others.

Theologoumenon: expression for a theological theory proposed by theologians, that does not belong to the deposit of faith; it is a theologoumenon to say, for example, that the Holy Spirit has assumed the human reality of Mary, making her human motherhood a divine motherhood.

Theology: in trinitarian language designates the Trinity in itself, abstracting from its manifestation in history; *theology* is contrasted with *economy.*

Trias: Greek expression to designate the trinity of Persons.

Also by Leonardo Boff

Cry of the Earth, Cry of the Poor

ISBN 1-57075-136-6

"The wisdom of Francis of Assisi, the cry of the poor,
and the power of earth's healing—all are gathered
together in this beautiful testament of hope."
—*Jay B. McDaniel*

Ecology & Liberation
A New Paradigm

ISBN 0-88344-978-1

"A book that will have profound implications
for earth and humanity's future. With his emphasis
on creation as the new paradigm, Boff's theology
has never been more liberating."
—*Matthew Fox*

Introducing Liberation Theology
Leonardo Boff and Clodovis Boff

ISBN 0-88344-550-6

"One of the finest explanations of liberation
in the English language."
—*Robert F. Drinan, s.j.*

Please support your local bookstore, or call 1-800-258-5838.

For a free catalogue, please write us at
Orbis Books, Box 308
Maryknoll NY 10545-0308
or visit our website at www.orbisbooks.com

Thank you for reading *Holy Trinity, Perfect Community*.
We hope you enjoyed it.